WINNING ♦ AT ♥ CASINO ♠ GAMBLING ♣

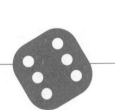
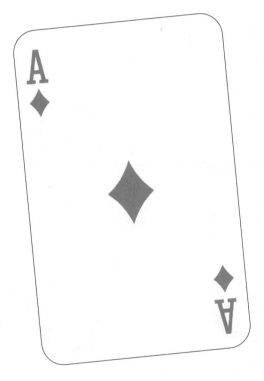

BOOKS ♦ BY ♥ LYLE ♠ STUART ♣

Casino Gambling for the Winner

God Wears A Bow Tie (a novel)

Inside Western Union (with M.J. Rivise)

Lyle Stuart on Baccarat

Mary Louise

The Secret Life of Walter Winchell

Winning at Casino Gambling

Lyle Stuart

BARRICADE BOOKS INC. New York, New York

Queries regarding rights and permissions should be addressed to

Barricade Books Inc.
150 Fifth Avenue
New York, NY 10011

Manufactured in the United States of America

Second Printing

Library of Congress Cataloging in Publication Data

Stuart, Lyle.
    Winning at casino gambling / by Lyle Stuart.
        p.   cm.
        ISBN 1-56980-012-X
    1. Gambling. 2. Baccarat. 3. Dice games. I. Stuart, Lyle. II. Title.
GV1301.S85   1994
795'.01—dc20   94-25585
                                                        CIP

This book is dedicated
to the most important ladies in my life:

my wondrous wife, Carole,

my loving and delightful daughter, Sandra Lee Stuart,

and my loving "no-stopping-her" stepdaughter,
Jenni Livingston

—and to the memory of Mary Louise.

I would be remiss if I failed to thank Eileen Brand for her tip-top editing job as well as the many people who helped improve the quality and accuracy of the information in this book by reading the manuscript and making their suggestions and corrections.

These are, (in strict alphabetical order!)

Xen Angelidis
Ed Becker
Arnold Boston
Bill Friedman
Jon Gilbert
Phil Juliano
Arnold Bruce Levy
Victor Lownes
Randy Meyerson
Howard Schwartz
John Smith
Carole Stuart
Larry Woolf

♠ C O N T E N T S ♣

INTRODUCTION

WAY BACK IN 1978, I wrote a book about casino gambling. It was written expressly for the man or woman who was determined to win.

It wasn't for those vast hordes of men and women who go to casinos for fun or who play games to "...only lose x-dollars" or to "make a donation."

The book was titled *Casino Gambling for the Winner* and it was eminently successful. It was the first savvy book on the subject, and I was the first writer who knew intimately of what he wrote. I was a player, and had been an investor in and owner of one point (1 percent) of a major Las Vegas casino.

Casino Gambling for the Winner became the largest-selling cloth book ever published on the subject. It sold more than 120,000 copies at $20. The mass-market paperback, for which Random House paid me an advance against royalties of $150,000, sold several hundred thousand copies.

BILLIONS OF QUARTERS have been dropped into casino slot machines since then. Now, sixteen years later, gambling is one of the fastest growing industries not just in the United States of America but throughout the world.

A FEW MONTHS AGO I entered the first International Invitational Baccarat Tournament sponsored by (Bally's) The Grand in Atlantic City. There were one hundred players from locations as far away as Venezuela, Indonesia and Hong Kong, I captured First Place for a total win of $125,000.

Fans of my first book told me it was time to write another.

IF YOU'RE ONE OF THE ninety-two million who annually visit casinos in Las Vegas, Reno, Laughlin, Atlantic City, Iowa, Colorado, Illinois, one of the 56 Mississippi Riverboats or the nearest native-American (Indian) reservation, and you go there for a good time, some good shows, some tennis or golf, some good food and drink and perhaps some extracurricular sex, this book isn't for you.

Rather, it's for that rare person who has some notion of what gambling is all about, wants to beat the casinos, and wants to know if this is at all possible.

It is.

I've been gambling in casinos since the mid-1950s, and from then until now I've been skeptical of people who offered to tell you their secrets about how to make millions in the stock market or how to win at the races. If *they* knew, why wouldn't they themselves do what they claim they can do instead of offering to share their "secrets" for a few paltry dollars?

ONE SUNNY DAY IN 1977, after years of frequenting casinos, I set a goal for myself. It was to win money on ten consecutive visits to Las Vegas. I did. In *Casino Gambling for the Winner* I gave the dates, named the casinos, and listed the amounts I won on each of my ten visits. (The eleventh visit was a disaster and I gave the details of that one too in my book.)

My total take-home win after all expenses was $166,505. This was after deducting First Class air fare (reimbursed by the casinos), food, drinks, hotel suites, car rentals, substantial tips for dealers and even the charge for parking my car at Kennedy Airport.

In terms of the dollar's buying strength then, this would equal about one million dollars today.

I told in detail how I did it. Since then, I've had several learning experiences, and I've learned much to add to the original picture I painted.

You hold in your hands a composite of what I knew then, and what I've experienced and learned in the seventeen years since.

I said in my first book that my initial instinct had been to make it impersonal—and even to publish under a pseudonym. But I decided that since it was going to be authentic and totally honest, I would put my name to it. This book, too, is a first-person chronicle all the way.

With no shyness or false modesty, let me tell you that what you are about to read will replace my original book as the most savvy book around on the subject. And probably, for you, the most valuable.

Lyle Stuart

Stuyvesant, New York
November, 1994

1

T H E B A S I C S

I'M ASSUMING YOU KNOW the basic rules of the casino games. If you don't, buy a five-dollar book somewhere and learn them. This is a university class; not a kindergarten.

If you know casino gaming, the following observation may be unnecessary for you. Think about it anyway. Let's end the Age of Innocence immediately by understanding this statement:

CASINO GAMES WERE NOT DESIGNED
TO FAVOR THE PLAYER.

It's critical, so read it several times. And *don't ever forget it*. Those people on the other side of the tables didn't build their billion-dollar palaces as contributions to the welfare of mankind. The casino games that give you pleasure were created to take your money.

"Doubt that the stars are fire; doubt that the sun doth move," as Prince Hamlet said to Ophelia, but do not doubt what you have just read.

The objective of every single game in the casino is to separate you from your money. Some games will take it from you more rapidly than others. They all, with the exception of a single wager in craps that I'll describe later, have the advantage of odds against you. It's called "the vig-orish" or "vig" or, as I shall refer to it, the percentage.

The Internal Revenue Service doesn't worry about get-ting its fair share of player winnings. Its gaming experts know that the big tax income will come from the casino side. They understand house percentages better than do most players.

THE PRESIDENT OF HARRAH'S, Phil Satre, recently told members of the National Press Club in Washington: "We aren't in [the casino] business to capitalize on com-pulsive behavior. We are in the business to entertain our customers."

Not!

If Harrah's had a way to remove money from its cus-tomers' pants pockets and purses while they were at home sleeping, do you think they would be heart-broken because they didn't "entertain" you?

Applesauce!

The "entertainment" is an ether, an anesthetic filled with eye-catching colorful graphics and dynamic, mind-reeling sounds, all designed to lull you into complacency while you are being separated from your bucks and to make you feel good before, while, and after it happens.

I much prefer the candor in what Vegas World Casino's egocentric Bob Stupak says in his statement that, "I target everybody. I'm in the business of taking their money. It makes no difference to me if it's a Social Security check, a welfare check or a stock dividend check. It's our duty to extract as much money from the customers as we can, and send them home with smiles on their faces."

Or, listen to what the manager of a famous Fremont Street casino told me several years ago: "Our objective is to separate the player from every dime he owns. We're not really doing our job unless the last check the customer cashes with us bounces for lack of funds."

CASINO EXECUTIVES DON'T much enjoy my telling you this. They prefer that you think of them as your smiling friends and good buddies. Forgive them. They have investments to protect and careers to pursue.

The wolf so loves the sheep that he eats him.

You've been warned!

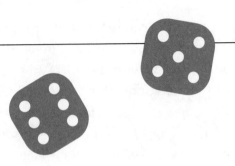

2

THE PERCENTAGES AGAINST YOU ON SLOTS

L ET'S TALK ABOUT PERCENTAGES and let's illustrate this point with a primitive dollar slot machine. Our imaginary machine is set to pay out 90 percent of everything it takes in. You insert a dollar and you could get back $25 or $2,500. But, over a period of time, the payoffs won't exceed 90 percent of all the dollars inserted. In theory, when you insert $10 you'll get $9 back. If you put that $9 into the machine, you'll get $8.10 back. If you insert the $8.10, you'll get back $7.29. And so forth until you've fed it all into the machine.

Now, obviously, dollar machines don't return dimes, nickels and pennies. Obviously, too, wins and losses are random so that you might put in $10 and win $100 or lose all $10. But if the machine is pegged to pay back 90 percent for every dollar inserted, the casino edge against you is 10 percent.

Robert Mazzocco, writing in *The New York Review of Books,* described the one-armed bandits in the casino as "stacked back-to-back like markers in a graveyard."

It's a lively graveyard.

Twenty years ago, no sophisticated gambler would ever be seen playing slots—not even those advertised as "The Hottest Slots in Town." Slots were designed for the mind-less player or for the wives and lady friends of gamblers who had time to kill while their husbands or boy friends did the "real" gambling at the tables. Slots were for people too lazy or too dull to learn the rules of even the simplest of the other games in the casino.

They tell about a man and woman in the casino-hotel elevator. He screams at her for dropping $200 at the slots. She's in tears. Suddenly she looks up and says, "Why are you so hard on me? I lost two hundred dollars but you lost $2,000 at craps."

"That's different," he says. "I know what I'm doing."

DESPITE THE HIGH purchase price and high license fees and taxes on slot machines, they were profitable even in the old days because there was so little human labor involved in keeping them running. Low-paid change personnel, a mechanic for repairs, and an occasional supervisor, made them ripe profit plums for every casino.

In 1977, the slots produced such a river of profit for the 269 casinos in Nevada at the time that 40.9 percent of Nevada's total taxable gambling revenue came from the slots.

In Atlantic City, where the first casino opened its doors in 1978, players were less sophisticated. Here, the slots got an even greater percentage of the gaming play. Females over the age of 45 were and are the backbone of slot machine play. At the end of 1979, three casinos were oper-

ating in that city-by-the-sea and they reported that 42 percent of their money came from their 3,434 slot machines.

Nevada has, at this writing, 147,586 slot machines in
operation. These include 169 1-cent machines and 91 that
require $100 tokens to play. Atlantic City has 25,438 slot
machines. These account for more than 50 percent of all
casino profits both in Nevada and in New Jersey.

Why?

Because something happened.

Someone invented the progressive slot machine. I
don't know the name of the genius who thought this one
up, but he deserves the Casino Congressional Medal of
Appreciation, if there were such a thing.

Now, for three quarters or three dollars you could win
millions.

Just three months ago, on August 13, 1994, a doctor
named Frank Oliveto drove from Port Jefferson, New
York, to Atlantic City. In the casino, he sat down at a blackjack table but immediately was asked to leave because he
had a lit cigar in his mouth and this was one of the growing number of "no smoking" tables.

Dr. Oliveto wanted to smoke his cigar, so he wandered
over to a *Megabucks* slot machine and deposited eighty
dollars tokens, three at a time. Suddenly, after ten minutes,
lights on the machine he was playing began to flash and
bells rang.

Said Oliveto: "I didn't understand what was happening
so I asked the people next to me how much I'd won. They
told me I'd won everything."

Oliveto had hit the *Megabucks* jackpot for exactly
$8,545,507.89. It was the largest slot win to date in Atlantic

City. (Oliveto, who was a bricklayer before becoming an orthopedic surgeon, says he'll do less cutting and more cigar smoking. He will be paid in twenty equal installments over twenty years, but so what? He can buy a lot of cigars with his $427,275.40 annual checks.)

The *Quartermania* jackpot in Atlantic City is currently bulging with more than one million dollars.

A man from Golden, Colorado, was visiting the small town of Mesquite, Nevada. He decided to invest ten dollars worth of quarters in the *Quartermania* machine in the Peppermill Hotel and Casino. He hit a $432,645 jackpot.

Megabucks in Nevada has a current jackpot of more than $4 million. Fifty-cent machines (*Fabulous 50s*) pay over $750,000. And, yes, several casinos even offer nickel progressives with jackpots of $75,000.

Megabucks and the related other banks of progressives are part of a system developed and operated by International Gaming Technology. In addition to Atlantic City (where 186 *Megabucks* are linked together in the twelve casinos), IGT runs separate but similar networks in Nevada, Colorado and even in far-away Macao.

Slots, which used to be your worst bet in the casino, have changed in many ways. There are poker machines, proliferating like rabbits. (Recently, I won $20,000 with a Royal Flush on a poker machine. This happened on a cruise ship named *Crystal Harmony* in a casino run by Caesars.)

The newest variety of slot machines don't even require change people. They feature the bill acceptor, invented only seven years ago. You insert your bills into the machine and the screen tells you how much credit you have. The

MGM Grand in Las Vegas, has this feature on all of their 3,512 machines. The Mirage in Las Vegas, features it on about half its machines and is phasing it in on the others. Some other casinos are using similar devices.

Nor need you any longer pull the machine handle (though you're free to do so if that's your preference) because most machines have the spin feature that does it all for you.

Slots work as they always have. They are not, as some people believe, "fixed" only to land on certain symbols at certain times. The fact is, you can hit a jackpot, and with the very next spin of the reels, hit it again.

3

MORE ABOUT SLOTS

Let me explain how slot machines work: If a machine contained only one reel and this reel had an equal number of cherries and pears and peaches, and a cherry paid back two coins, a cherry would come up once in three times. The machine would thus pay off 33 1/3 percent and give the casino a 66 2/3 percent profit.

Imagine that there are two reels. The possible combinations would be (1) cherry and cherry; (2) cherry and peach; (3) cherry and pear; (4) pear and peach; (5) pear and pear; (6) pear and cherry; (7) peach and peach; (8) peach and pear; (9) peach and cherry. Over a period of time, two cherries would come up once in nine times. There are three symbols and two reels so the mathematics is 3 x 3.

Imagine now a slot machine with four reels and 80 symbols on each reel. The jackpot symbol on a progressive may appear once on each reel. The chance of getting a jackpot symbol on all four reels on the same line is 80 x 80 x 80 x 80. Thus, the odds against all four jackpot symbols coming up on the same line are one in 40,960,000.

In the past, teams of cheats would figure out ways of stealing from the machines. They'd use magnets, drill into the machines and commit all manner of diabolical maneuvers to beat the machines dishonestly.

Those days are history.

Most machines operating today are governed by a computer chip known as the random number generator (RNG). This chip controls the machine. It cycles through numbers and produces the combinations you see on the screen.

The RNG isn't concerned with whether you play one coin or three. If you play only one coin and a progressive jackpot appears for which you needed to insert three coins,—the machine didn't do this deliberately, contrary to what some shocked players believe after it happens to them.

The RNG runs all the time in some machines. In others, it is activated only when you insert your first coin.

Never play a progressive machine with less than the maximum number of coins. Otherwise you deprive yourself of your big chance, the dream-filled chance at winning one of those rich jackpots.

How are the payout percentages determined? The casino decides what percentage it will pay out. When it orders a machine, it tells the manufacturer exactly what percentage it wants the machine to pay back.

Some slot managers prefer machines that pay out small amounts often. You get lots of 2, 5, and 10 coin winners. This approach often acts as flypaper for the innocent. Sit there a little longer. You'll lose a little more.

Given their percentages against you is the reason that, in the future, every slot machine will have its own stool. Sit. Be comfortable. Your host wants to induce you to stay longer. Watch the lights. Hear the bells. Listen to the coins drop with their resonance in the trays of nearby slots. You won't always hear coins because technology has created what are called "coinless" or "coin-free" slots. You insert a card on which the bar-code tells the machine how much credit you have. Too, bill validators that take paper money are proliferating so quickly that some casinos already are taking in 30 percent of their slot income in paper.

The payoffs are markedly different in different parts of town. The law in Nevada is that the slots need pay out only 75 percent of what you insert. Actually, most machines are programmed to pay out 90 percent or more. In Atlantic City, by law, the slots must pay out 83 percent. Again, the average they pay is more nearly 90 percent. (Reno slots are fixed to pay about 1 percent more than Las Vegas slots.)

In June 1994, the New Jersey Casino Control Commission reported that Showboat's $25 machines in Atlantic City paid out $100.50 for every $100 inserted. Not to be outdone, Trump Castle's $100 machines paid out $108 for every $100 inserted.

In addition to the fascination of the lights, sound and colors, some casinos now add smell. Yes, they're acting on confirmed studies which show that a pleasant-smelling vapor, sprayed into the slot machine area, will cause customers to insert as much as 50 percent more money!

In the old days, to add to the sense of excitement and keep the player at the machine, some slots were programmed so their jackpot symbols often appeared just above or below the payoff line. This was called the "near-miss illusion" and was outlawed in Nevada in 1989.

THE PROMINENT psychologist Frederic (B.F.) Skinner once trained a white rat to become a slot machine player. The rat discovered that when he pulled a chain with his teeth, a marble would drop out of a box. The rat learned to insert the marble into a slot which would then eject a tiny piece of dog biscuit. The interesting (to me) part is that when the machine was set so the rat got the dog biscuit only occasionally instead of every time he inserted the marble, he played more often. This is the kind of dedication the casinos love to develop in their slot players who get as excited about near-misses as they do about small payoffs.

This reminds me of a remark made by casino owner Bob Stupak. Stupak boasted "When I bring fifty additional machines into Vegas World, I consider them fifty more mousetraps. You need a mousetrap to catch a mouse."

What's the key to beating the slots?

It's simple.

Quit when you're ahead!

4

KENO AND ROULETTE

Slots are not the worst gamble in a casino. Keno is a dol-lar-grabber. It can take a 25 percent slice of your investment. (The payoff for correctly picking a single num-ber is 3-to-1 but the odds against you are 4-to-1.) That's why the Keno parlor offers so many comfortable chairs with armrests.

Keno is a game that is going to pay a big chunk of the cost of those elegant chandeliers and (where they still fea-ture them) those flashy neon signs. Atlantic City casinos have added Keno to their roster of games, although in Las Vegas the belief is that it's a dying game.

Do people win at Keno? Does anyone really win $25,000 for an investment of a dollar or two? Sure. When Milton Prell opened the Aladdin in Las Vegas, one man won $10,000 four times within 24 hours. Improbable, you say? Yes, but it happened. (We'll deal with the improbable later in this book.)

The owners of the Aladdin were disturbed but not dis-tressed. They knew that, in time, they would win all that money back. They did.

Before computers came of age, winning numbers would be drawn from a bowl full of Ping-Pong balls. A fellow I know spent 24 hours without sleep in a downtown Las Vegas casino because he wanted to find out if he could beat the game. Keeping careful records, he observed that, despite the fact that the Ping-Pong balls were washed twice weekly, some balls tended to appear more often than others.

He played only those numbers that came up most often. During those 24 hours he literally played thousands of combinations. He won some money, but he failed to hit the "big" one. He never played Keno again.

One day to entertain my then-12-year-old son, Rory, while my wife and I played craps, I told him about my friend's findings. Rory was impressed. So we sat him on a couch in the lobby of a casino-hotel to keep records while watching the Keno screen above the hotel's registration desk.

After several games had been played, Rory's records showed some repeaters. I let him select a one-number-card, a 4-number card, etc. The combination cost me $22.50.

Twenty minutes later I walk back to the lobby to check on him.

"Any luck, Rory?"

"Nah," he said. "Not one number came up."

"Let's try them again," I suggested. I invested another $22.50, and we duplicated the cards he'd just played.

Fifteen minutes later, a casino host tapped me on the shoulder. "Mr. S., you'd better come with me to the lobby," he said. "Your son just won some Keno money."

He'd won $2,300. And to this day he's never repaid my $45 investment!

THERE ARE LOTS of other games in casinos to avoid. You don't want to play The Big Wheel which gives the casino 15 percent or better odds. You don't want to play Red Dog which has a 20-to-40 percent house advantage. You don't want to play Pai Gow or Pai Gow Poker or Caribbean Stud or any of the other cutsie, often complicated, newcomers.

Next to Keno, the worst major established game in a casino is American roulette. That's the one where the table has both an "0" and an "00," and the odds are 5.26 percent against you.

Or look at it this way: with its added double zero, the casino short-changes you $2 every time you win. The true odds are 1 in 38. You get paid 35 for your 1. That's 35 plus the chip you wagered.

Roulette is a slow game. It has fewer decisions per hour than most other games.

I wrote previously, "If you favor roulette, save your air fare and mail the casino a check for your probable loss." Since then, as players have become more sophisticated, some casinos also offer a wheel with a single "0." At least on these, the percentage against you is reduced to 2.7 percent. If you can't find one of the single zero tables, find another game to play.

And here, for the first time, I'll reveal a roulette strategy that has worked for me. I learned it from my friend, Arnold Boston, a retired dentist-turned-magician who is widely known as "Doc."

First, unless a wheel is faulty (and casino supervisors spot and replace these quickly) you can be certain that every number will come out about as often as every other number.

In some German casinos, where roulette is the primary game, careful records are kept and monthly bulletins are for sale that report the number of times each number has appeared during the previous month. They might read thusly:

#1. 42,867

#2. 42,578

#3. 42,901

Etc.

To repeat what I said before, every number comes up approximately the same number of times. But—and this is the big "but"—each number doesn't come up once in every 38 spins of the wheel. Some numbers don't appear for hours. Some numbers repeat. (I recently watched 27 come up five times in a row!)

This is what "Doc" Boston does. He waits and watches until five numbers have come up. Then he places small bets on each of them. On the next roll, he bets the first four again but eliminates the last number and substitutes the one that has just won. Gradually, after every few spins, he becomes progressive, doubling his wager on each number. I've watched him walk away a winner again and again.

ODDS ARE THE KEY to all gaming. Therefore, always seek the wagers that most favor you. A chip on one number (called *Plein* or Straight Up) pays 35-to-1 (the real odds are 38-to-1). Some players believe you give the casino an additional advantage by placing one chip on two numbers (*Cheval* or Split) where, if one of the two comes up, you are only paid 17-to-1. They believe the worst bet, of course, is the *Transversal simple* or six-line bet. You bet on six numbers with one chip and if any of the six wins, you are paid 5-to-1. So now, they say, you're only getting paid at the rate of 30-to-1 instead of 35-to-one.

They're wrong, of course. The house edge is always and only those two extra numbers. Same thing for Odd vs. Even or Black vs. Red. The thing they ignore in their wrong thinking is that when you bet a cheval or any other combination and win, you get back your losing bet too. Thus when they pay you 17-to-1, they are actually still paying you 35 half chips plus the 1/2 chip that was on the losing number plus your winning half chip too. Net, 1/2 of what you'd collect if you'd bet a full chip on a winning number.

IN WHAT SEEMS LIKE two centuries ago, when I was a novice, I had an incredibly lucky experience on my first visit to the Casino De Paris in Monte Carlo. I *thought* I'd lost the equivalent of more than $100 on a single 2-to-1 bet on the bottom twelve numbers. (This is a wager on the 12 numbers at the top, middle or bottom dozen and is called a *Douzaine* or Dozen bet.)

I hurried across the casino floor to the cashier's cage to trade my American dollars for more French francs. When I returned to the roulette table, I learned that my wager had won, had won again, and had won a third time. I thought I had been playing the *bottom* dozen and instead I'd accidentally bet on the *top* dozen. I picked up chips worth more than $2,700 for a profit of $2,600.

My experience was dumb beginner's luck. But it failed to endear roulette to me, even European-style.

CHARLES DEVILLE WELLS inspired the song, *The Man Who Broke the Bank at Monte Carlo*, by winning £50,000 in two days and nights at the tables. He wound up serving eight years in prison for fraud, and when he died in Paris in 1926, he was penniless.

THERE ARE STILL ONLY three serious casino games: baccarat, blackjack and craps. Most of these pages will be devoted to craps and baccarat. These are my favorite table action because they offer the best shot a casino will give you, retaining the smallest percentage. They require no counting, no cheating, no "smart guy" stuff.

But since it continues to be the most popular table game, we'll talk first about blackjack.

5

THE SERIOUS GAMES

If you are a mathematical genius, who has a sharp eye and a marvelous memory, you'll incline toward blackjack. The game has become progressively more popular, especially with men under the age of 45. One needn't be a brain surgeon or a rocket scientist to count to 21.

Technically, the casino game is called "21," for in the true game of blackjack, the first person dealt a total of 21 in two cards becomes the new dealer or banker. In casino-style "21," the casino always deals.

FIVE YEARS AGO, when I sold Lyle Stuart Inc. for 12 million dollars, I had become the largest distributor of gaming books in the world. I was the proud publisher of *Playing Blackjack as a Business* by Lawrence Revere and *Blackjack Your Way to Riches* by Richard Albert Canfield —the best two books on the subject after Thorp. I also published such gems as Bill Friedman's *Casino Management* (I priced this at a hefty $125 a copy) which sold out several printings and became the "Bible" for aspiring casino executives.

My wife Carole and I organized a new company, Barricade Books. (We started with a third partner, Allen G. Schwartz, but he had to sell his interest back to us early 1994 when President Clinton appointed him a Federal judge.)

Barricade Books has now published the first really sound book on playing blackjack with multiple decks. Its author is Edward Early and is titled *The Ultimate Blackjack Book* (Playing Blackjack with Multiple Decks) and it retails for $12.

ONE OF MY AUTHORS, Ken Uston, took a case to the New Jersey State Supreme Court and won the right of counters to play in Atlantic City.

Nevada casinos can still legally ban them.

Uston was determined to keep suing Nevada casinos until he got a favorable ruling. Unfortunately, he died somewhat mysteriously in a Paris hotel in 1987.

Incidentally, I disagree with those who say counters shouldn't be allowed to play. The casino can easily outfox the counters by allowing only half of each four or six-deck shoe to be dealt and by instructing the dealer to shuffle the cards any time a player more than doubles his wager. For example, if any player at the table bets $100 and his or her previous wager was $25, the dealer can halt the game and shuffle.

There are other conditions. A casino can ask anyone to leave the table who doesn't bet every hand—and seems to be counting and waiting for the deck to become picture-rich. A new wrinkle these days is to have designated tables where you must be there at the beginning because new-comers can't enter the game after the first hand of a shoe is dealt.

It's against the law for you to have a hidden computer on your body when you play. But no law prevents the casino from using a computer. Some casinos have installed them in the "eye in the sky" department. When a dealer or supervisor suspects a player of being a card counter, he phones upstairs. Focusing a telescopic lens on the table, the security man programs into the computer every play made by the suspected counter. It determines whether he's a counter or is just running lucky. If the former, in Nevada, and elsewhere, he is asked to leave and is told that his play is no longer welcome in that casino.

LOTS OF TIME is consumed by dealers mixing cards. The more often they shuffle, the fewer hands they can deal each hour, and fewer hands equal less casino profits.

Dealers are instructed to deal 60 or more hands an hour. Accordingly, they are supposed to shuffle six decks in 80 seconds. Shuffling can eat up eight rounds of playing time an hour. Remember that the more hands dealt, the better for the casino since the odds favor the house.

Books have been written for the professional gambler telling how to have someone peek at the dealer's hole card from the other side the pit and then signal to a confeder-ate at the table. (The move is called "spooking".) All this pretty much went down the chute with the introduction of a feature on all new blackjack tables. It's a reflector that allows dealers to see their down card if their open card is an ace. They slide the corner of the down card under it and only they can see its denomination.

Counters?

On one notable occasion, a counting team occupied an entire table. The casino clocked them. The team produced average winnings of less than $25 an hour.

Less than twenty-five dollars an hour!

Is it worth all the turmoil, tension, planning, and risk to keep counters from playing? Is it worth all the time/profits lost doing all those extra shuffles?

I say "No."

AFTER THE PUBLICATION of my first book, I received several complaints from acknowledged blackjack experts such as Allan N. Wilson, author of the out-of-print classic, *The Casino Gambler's Guide,* saying that I was too dismissive about blackjack.

So, here are several chapters on the game and in the next, I'll present you with a simple basic strategy for non-counters.

They say that card-counters win consistently at blackjack. Not the ones I've played with. I've personally known and sat beside many card-counters from Mannie Kimmel and Stanley Roberts to Ken Uston and Lawrence Revere himself. I have yet to meet one who wins *consistently.* Counting may invert percentages, but it doesn't control the critical element of luck. Even the best counters win some and lose some.

I know one counter who thought he had them fooled. He worked up a stake of more than $40,000 in winnings in long bouts at the tables. Then his wife refused to join him for dinner, and this so upset him that, on returning to a blackjack table, he lost $80,000 within a short time.

6

BLACKJACK AND A STRATEGY

Dear Reader,

I promised you a simple blackjack strategy for people who don't count cards. I shall keep you in suspense no longer. Here is my *non-counting* blackjack strategy.

This basic strategy doesn't require great memory. For you need count only the cards in your own hand. Since single-deck games are now found in very few casinos, the following is designed for four, six and eight-deck shoes.

You should play only in casinos where the dealer must stop on *any* 17. Some casinos allow the dealer to draw to a soft 17 (ace and 6). This is to your disadvantage. Never gamble where you have an extra disadvantage to overcome.

Note the dealer's up card. Everything you do is based on that card.

If the dealer shows an 8, 9, 10, or ace, the realistic approach is to recognize that since 18-1/2 is the average winning hand, you can't stop at 12, 13, 14, 15, or 16 but

41

must try to get into that "safe zone" between 17 and 21. So hit your hand until you get 17 or better. Or break.

If, on the other hand, the dealer's up card is 4, 5, or 6, you should stop on a hard hand of 12, 13, 14, 15, or 16. There is no point in breaking (going over 21) when the dealer also has a chance of breaking.

Remember, the game is equal in every way except that if you get Blackjack, you win one-and-one-half times your wager. So the only house advantage is when you break and then the dealer breaks. You have the same hands but they aren't "pushes" (in which neither side wins) because the dealer takes your money *before* he breaks. (A dealer will break an average of 28 times for every hundred hands dealt.)

I didn't instruct you on what to do when your two cards total 12 or 13. These are hands where you will break and lose if you buy a 10 or 9 respectively. You stay on them *except* when the dealer also shows a 2 or 3. In such a situation, he or she has more potential than would be true with a 4, 5, or 8—so you shouldn't feel content. Against a 2 or a 3, your move is arbitrary. You could sit tight or you could draw one card and stop (if you haven't "broken") no matter what the new total of your hand.

Let's talk about "soft" hands. These are an ace paired with a 2, 3, 4, 5, 6, 7, 8, or 9. Forget ace-8 or ace-9, because there is nothing the dealer could show that would ever cause you to draw. These two are automatic stop-where-you-are hands.

Ace-2 is probably the worst of the soft hands for the Player, but if the dealer shows a 5 or 6, it is still a good double-down. (If a dealer shows a 4 in a single-deck game that's also a good double-down but not in a multiple-deck game.)

Ace-6 is a powerfully good double-down against the dealer's 3, 4, 5 or 6. The reason it's so strong is that the dealer has an excellent probability of going over 21. There are many cards that will improve an ace-6 and nothing that really hurts, because, unless the dealer breaks, there is no way you can win with an ace-6. All you can hope to do with 17 is to tie. So no matter what the dealer shows, you *never* stand with an ace-6. It's the one hand you always try to improve.

An ace-7 is also a good double-down against a dealer's 5 or 6. Against a lower dealer's card, it's best not to double-down. Just stand with your 18.

This may be hard to grasp. However, it has been proven out by millions of computer-tested hands. When a dealer shows a 9 or 10 and you have an ace-7 (a soft 18), you automatically hit. I can hear you moaning, "But the only thing that can help me is an ace, 2, or 3!"

True. But believe me, although you will lose many hands, you will win more. The theory is that if you had 18 every hand, you would be an automatic loser, but with 19 every time you'd be an automatic winner.

Always double-down on 11, no matter what card the dealer shows. Even if he or she turns over a blackjack, you get your double-down money back, and you have a slight edge by doubling down against an ace.

Two 5s is always a double-down hand and never a split. Always double-down any total of 10 except against an ace or 10.

A 9 can be doubled-down against a 3, 4, 5, or 6. Don't double-down a total of 9 except in the above examples.

What about splitting pairs? The rule used to be "Never split 10s," but there are those who believe that splitting 10s against 4, 5 or 6 is a good wager. *Always* split aces.

Sit with a pair of 9s against a dealer's 10 or ace. Split 9s against a 9 or any number below it. I know you'll resist this because you're sitting with 18, but believe me, it's the proper move. Split 9s against an 8. Don't split two 8s against a 7. The dealer either has 17 or may bust.

Automatically split 9s against 3, 4, 5, or 6. Split 9s against a 2 only if you are allowed to double-down after a split. (Know your casino's rules: some casinos allow this and some don't.)

"SURRENDER" IS a comparatively recent feature. Early surrender means that when the dealer is ready to deal a third card to you, you announce "surrender" and the dealer takes your cards but leaves you with half your bet. Surrender 15 or 16 against a 9, 10, or ace. The reason is that the number of cards that can improve your 15 or 16 are so few that you're better off getting back half of your wager. Casinos should offer you surrender. If they don't, and another nearby casino does, play at the one that does.

A recent addition to the options is that when you have blackjack and the dealer shows an ace, you can accept even money, in which case you get dollar-for-dollar for your bet whether or not the dealer has a blackjack. Or you can insure your hand, which means that if you bet $10 and insure it for $5 and the dealer has blackjack, you get back $10 for your $5 and your hand is a push. If the dealer doesn't have blackjack, you lose your $5 but get $15 for your blackjack.

Or you can refuse even money, not take insurance, and risk having the dealer also show blackjack and you collect nothing. This is what I do. Sure, you lose some. But the percentages say that on balance, you'll collect that 1.5 times your wager more often than not.

NEW GAMES are introduced all the time. A recent one called "Let It Ride" permits you to take back most of your wager after the cards are dealt. Then, of course, there's the one where the dealer deals all the cards open (face up) including his own. The catch is that the casino compensates for this by winning all ties.

Believe that old adage: There ain't no free lunch!

7

F I R S T V I S I T

W hen I flew to casino-land for the first time, it was so long ago that our plane was propeller-driven and it took eight hours to reach Las Vegas from New York. I really didn't go to gamble. I was on my way to Beverly Hills with my first wife, my daughter and my infant son. We made a stopover in Vegas for three days because Broadway columnist Paul Denis had told me to.

"You've got to visit Las Vegas," he said. "It's the way the world is going to end."

That intrigued me.

The year was 1957. Joe E. Lewis was starring in the show at El Rancho Vegas (later to burn down in a mysterious fire in 1960) and the show featured the incredibly beautiful dancer-stripper-porn star Candy Barr. Most of the major casinos of today didn't exist. There was a place called Sans Souci ("without care") which became the Castaways and which occupied land that is now part of the site of The Mirage.

The New York mob opened a very fancy hotel which they named Tropicana. It was designed for the so-called blue bloods, those people with fancy names, furs, fortunes and family pedigrees. They were invited and they did, indeed, flock to the opening: The Astors and the Vanderbilts and the Whitneys chatted with each other and observed the elegant casino.

The surroundings were lush. The food was excellent. Everybody was happy except the Tropicana owners. Until they experienced those first low-gross nights, they hadn't realized that blue bloods are not, as a class, heavy gamblers.

Other mistakes were made. A few years later, a plush watering hole was built on Las Vegas Boulevard South for millionaires who didn't care to gamble. It was called Tally-Ho. It boasted that it had no casino. It was built in English Tudor-style but with no deep thought given to its purpose. Why, for example, would a non-gambling millionaire want to visit Las Vegas? At that time, Vegas offered little more than sand, heat and hookers.

After two groups of owners dropped large sums of money on the no-brainer concept, Milton Prell bought the Tally-Ho and converted it into the Aladdin. And I became one of the owners or, as they used to say, "point holders."

But back to my first visit in 1957. I booked my wife and two children into The Tropicana. I didn't know the rules of the casino games. I didn't understand casino craps. Blackjack seemed simple enough but it would be years before I learned the strategy I just passed on to you.

I played blackjack.

Each hand called for thought and a decision. Of course it was a losing situation, and I lost $1,500.

Mary Louise enjoyed the surroundings and my two children played poolside next to Eddie Fisher and Debbie Reynolds* and their two children. The meals were good. I was impressed by knowing that, since nothing but cactus and grass grew in Las Vegas, every bite of food had to be flown, trained or trucked into the city.

In those days, an "All You Can Eat" buffet offered at least half-a-hundred different food choices and was available for $1.50. Liquor in the casinos was free. Rooms were moderately priced, and in our suite there was a beautiful bouquet of flowers (imported) to welcome us.

There were no traffic lights on Las Vegas Boulevard (the "Strip") and not much traffic. To the east and west of the Strip there was very little except barren land.

THINGS HAVE CHANGED. Today we live in the entertainment decade. And high on top of the entertainment pyramid is the casino. Las Vegas is now truly the Entertainment Capital of the World. It's America's major destination resort. Nearly 30 million people flock there each year, drawn by the new themed casino palaces. Gamblers bring their husbands, wives and children and their grandmothers and their friends for a good time. And new casinos continue to spring up from the desert offering everything you can imagine and some things you can't.

Roller coasters are being built at a cost of anywhere from two to fifteen million dollars.

---

*Debbie Reynolds now owns her own casino in Las Vegas.

Virtual Reality shows offer simulation experiences unequaled anywhere. Top casino leaders spend sleepless nights trying to figure what the public wants. Casino owner Steve Wynn builds what he wants and expects the public to love it.

Gaming, once considered something outside of good society is now part of not just American pop culture but of world culture.

Casinos in America have taken first place over Hollywood, television, books, cable-TV, videos, CDs, computers, magazines, and you-name-it. Americans now spend billions a year on gambling. The "drop" (the amount gambled) on commercial gambling games in 1993 was more than $394 billion dollars. The "hold" (gross gambling revenue retained by the casinos) exceeded $34.7 billion. That dwarfs what is spent on movie admissions—even with the tickets in some places as high as $8 per.

That $394 billion-dollar figure may already be obsolete when you read this, for casino gambling in America isn't growing, it's exploding! Indian reservations, Mississippi riverboats, and state-licensed monopolies like the one in New Orleans, mean that our society has given its imprimatur to gambling. Gaming's negative stereotype has all but disappeared.

It wasn't always this way. Puritanical attitudes about gambling were epidemic in the late 1880s and clung to our culture until the late 1960s. I know that when I visited Las Vegas for the first time, the players were mostly Italians and Jews from the big cities. Broadway-types, Damon Runyon-types, swinging businessmen, shady characters comprised most of the mix.

Few dreamed that gambling would ever become so accepted and respectable that even church groups and ladies' garden societies would get together for those exciting three-day Las Vegas junkets.

The fact is that it shocked and disturbed many when the first state lottery was launched on March 12, 1964. New Hampshire's Governor John King* bought the first ticket in a glitzy publicized ceremony. Today the lottery business is a 25-billion-dollar-a-year industry and lotteries are conducted in nearly 40 states. And I happen to believe it was the introduction of the legal lottery that led to casino gambling becoming an acceptable form of recreation.

Incidentally, nothing in gambling so exploits the gambler as the lottery. It takes a 50 percent cut of every lottery dollar spent. And the chance of picking a 6-number lotto winner is one in 14 million!

As Mike Orkin wrote: "State lotteries are the only game in some towns and not the only game in other towns but they are the worst game in all towns."

BY THE YEAR 2000, 95 percent of all Americans will live within a two-to-three-hour drive of a gambling casino. Studies have shown that distance plays a major role in gambling habits. The closer one lives to a casino, the more often one is likely to visit and gamble in one.

_____

*Contrast King's action against the recent refusal of Alaska's Governor Walter Hickel who vetoed a bill allowing cruise ships to operate their casinos while in Alaskan waters. He announced as he vetoed the bill, "I'm opposed to gambling because it adds nothing to civilization."

"Bugsy" Siegel had a dream of a gambling Mecca, legal and free of Government harassment. Del Webb saw himself building an entire gambling city. Webb once lunched with Siegel and suddenly turned pale when "Bugsy" chatted about killing some people. "Bugsy" noticed this and attempted to reassure his lunch companion by saying, "Don't worry, Mr. Webb, we only kill each other." (That declaration became the title of one of his biographies.)

But Siegel in his wildest dreams couldn't have dreamed an MGM Grand or a Mirage or a Treasure Island. None of the early mobster pioneers foresaw what has happened. Not gangster Frank Costello whom I interviewed in the Waldorf-Astoria Hotel barber shop and found him a pompous jerk. Not imaginative rough-tough pioneer and true gambler Benny Binion, who thought nothing of killing a customer if the customer created a disturbance in his place. Not shrewed former New York bookmaker Sandy Waterman, nor businessman Milton Prell, nor erudite Carl Cohen, nor colorful often-shot-at-but-never-killed Ash Resnick. Nor Gus Greenbaum, stabbed to death with his wife ("but at least we did it in another state") nor that certain mobster of whom Arnold Rothstein's former bodyguard, Charles "Toolie" Kandell told me, "It was a bum rap. Sure, he may have murdered five or six guys but he *never* dealt in dope!"

Ed Becker has been a Las Vegas resident from the time Gus Greenbaum hired him to do public relations for the Flamingo. Becker recalls that Greenbaum walked in and took control of the Flamingo on the night "Bugsy" Siegel was killed and before word of his death had gotten back to Las Vegas.

Some were visionaries of sorts. Some were bean counters and bottom line examiners and some were bold builders. But, with the exception of Webb and Prell, they'd grown up on the other side of the law and those early casino money harvest made Las Vegas feel like a Paradise to them.

THE MUSTACHES are gone. Their grandchildren may be involved in gaming but, if so, they toe a straight line. Gaming is no Mom and Pop stuff. It's a huge industry. Bigger than U.S. Steel. Bigger than General Motors. Bigger than Hollywood. Bigger than movies or liquor or cigarettes.

Of course, casino owners will argue that movies hold 100 percent of the "drop" and sell a lot of popcorn while casinos hold "only" 12 to 14 percent of the "drop" and have to comp a lot. But don't knock yourself out organizing a charity event on their behalf!

WHEN ONE WRITES a book that contains casino gaming specifics, it is doomed to become rapidly dated. So understand that by the time you read much of what I write here, things may already have changed.

For example, the MGM Grand in Las Vegas is, at this writing, the largest resort hotel in Las Vegas. There's a larger one in the Orient, and Foxwoods, the Mashantucket Indian reservation in Connecticut, occupies more space and contains more slot machines. Their credit cards that you show when you want a marker are marked "Wampum."

The tribe gathered plenty of wampum in 1993, showing a profit of more than $400 million. This comes to 1-1/3 million a year income for every man, woman and child of the 300-member tribe. Pity the poor Indians! (They'll accept you as a member of the tribe if you can prove your great-great-grandfather was a member of the tribe so that you have 1/16th Pequot blood.)

The man currently running Foxwoods is G. Michael Brown. No, he's not an Indian. Rather, he's an attorney who formerly directed the gambling enforcement division of the New Jersey State Attorney General's office. When the Pequots won the right to run a full casino, they couldn't raise financial backing. Twenty-three institutional lenders turned them down. Brown, having represented in his private law practice, Genting International, a Malaysian casino operating company, was able to obtain a $40 million loan.

Meanwhile, the Oneida tribe has opened Turning Point Casino in Verona, New York and has announced they deal single deck blackjack and welcome card-counters.

In Minneapolis, eleven tribes are running seventeen tribal casinos. There are now 142 native-American gaming centers of which 52 are full-facility gambling casinos. They pay no Federal tax and are generally immune from government regulations: city, state or national. Nor need they report, as publicly-owned casinos do, to the Securities & Exchange Commission.

Pretty lucky, these native Americans. At long last.

IN LAS VEGAS, the Sands was originally the "class" place to stay. They used to give me a spacious penthouse suite on the 18th floor. Then along came Caesars Palace and the Sands became déclassé. Now the "in" place is the Mirage.

Places like the Mirage, the MGM Grand, the Excalibur, Treasure Island and the Luxor have made Las Vegas an adult Disneyland that you have to see and experience to believe. More people visit Las Vegas each year than visit Orlando.

The Tropicana features a five-acre water-park and dozens of exotic birds and fish.

The MGM Grand sits on 112 acres and boasts a 33-acre theme park. It houses four casinos under one roof and these are on 175,000 square feet. Larry Woolf, MGM Grand's President, doesn't worry about competition from the riverboats or from the Indian casinos. Woolf believes that Las Vegas will do it "bigger, better, and with class."

The new MGM Grand show-spectacular cost 40 million dollars to launch. Awesome? Balance that against the fact that the MGM Grand offers its T-shirts for $20 and sells one million of them each year. That's $20,000,000. (The MGM Grand expects its retail shops to provide 4 percent of its total revenue.)

The Mirage's 54-foot-high man-made volcano erupts every half hour for three minutes. The lobby houses rare white tigers and, when you check in, you face a 53-foot-long 20,000-gallon saltwater tank in which swim sharks and hundreds of exotic fish from remote places in the world.

Treasure Island spent millions of dollars so it could present the Cirque du Soleil in a show called *Mysteré*. It is a fabulous, fabulous show unlike anything you've ever seen on any stage.

Skywalks link the Tropicana, the MGM Grand, the Excalibur and the Luxor. A monorail will link the MGM Grand with Bally's—almost a mile away.

Bob Stupak is close to completing construction of the world's highest tower.

New York-New York, a $300 million resort, is to be built by Kirk Kerkorian on 18 acres at the northwest corner intersection of the Strip and Tropicana Road. The 2,000-room hotel will be a joint venture for his MGM Grand and Primadonna Resorts.

The gags have already started. To give it a New York feeling, instead of a volcano or a pirate battle, New York-New York will feature a mugging every half-hour. Retail merchandise will be sold out of briefcases at every corner and a 3-card-Monte game will be used to hustle the marks in the hotel corridors. And, in the casino, when you ask for another card at blackjack, the dealer will say, "Fuck you! You've already got all da cards ya gonna get from me!"

8

MEMORIES OF AN EARLY DISASTER

On that first visit to Vegas in 1957 I lost $1,500. It was about half the cash reserve I had in the world. I thought about it and decided that rather than concern myself with the loss, I would concentrate on raising my income.

I did.

As time passed, I determined to learn the rules of the games. It has always amazed me that a person will spend years getting an education in order to develop a skill that will produce good income and then will visit a gambling casino and blow away a large chunk of that good income on games in which that person has almost zero knowledge.

I acquired some understanding. As the years sped by, the level of my wagers increased. I became a "high roller" and was given the special courtesies that high rollers receive and deserve.

I was "comped" wherever I chose to stay.

"Comped" means that First Class airline tickets, a luxury suite, the finest available food, liquor, the best seats at the shows, etc., are compliments of the house. The theory is that if you stay at *their* hotel you are more than likely to pay for it all at their tables. Even those who wander from casino to casino usually do at least 60 percent of their gaming in the casino of the hotel in which they sleep.

In those early days, my losses were high. So were my wins. I lost as much as $30,000 in five minutes and won as much as $60,000 in ten.

LUCK IS A lady but—as with all ladies of class—she chooses her lovers imperiously. Let me cite a single complete experience. It requires a little background.

Milton Prell got his start in gambling many years ago when he bought a near-bankrupt bingo parlor in Gardena, California. He examined the operation. Shills were being handed the winning bingo cards in advance.

"Fire the shills," he ordered, after buying the bingo parlor. "From now on we're going to really give the prizes to the players."

Fire the shills? This was heresy!

"You can't do that," his manager protested. "We'll go broke in five weeks."

"We'll go broke in six weeks the way we're going now," Prell told him.

In time, Prell's place won the reputation of being the only honest bingo parlor in town. It thrived. Eventually Prell came to Las Vegas. With some financial assistance from his brother-in-law, Gil Gilbert, he launched the Sahara and the Mint—and built fine reputations for both casinos while he owned them.

When Milton Prell bought the Tally-Ho to convert it to the Aladdin, he invited me to join him, so I invested one percent (one point) needed to buy and open the hotel-casino. Prell had the reputation for being honest. The story around town was that while most joints kept three sets of books (one for the stockholders, one for the IRS, and the real one) Prell kept only two.

Owning one percent seemed like a good investment and a fun one. I could point to the thousands of light bulbs outside the hotel-casino and say with pride, "I own one out of every hundred of those!"

To qualify, I was required to list my every asset and its origins on voluminous questioneers. There were long forms for Clark County and longer forms for Nevada. After I filled out and submitted the papers, the Aladdin, gave me "sky's the limit" credit. (Which is part of the story that follows.)

At that time I was about to publish a biography of Howard Hughes by a former *Time* magazine writer named Ezra Goodman. Attempts were being made to halt, or, at the very least, delay its publication.

I was invited to a meeting at a townhouse on New York's East Side (rented from an actress named Faye Emerson who had married Elliott Roosevelt, the son of President Franklin Delano Roosevelt). There, Hollywood attorney Greg Bautzer, representing Hughes, spoke in terms of "rewarding" me with as much as two hundred thousand dollars.

Being young, gutsy, and bursting with idealism and integrity—I explained that I would defy anyone who tried to buy me off, bully me off or frighten me off. Bautzer then proposed a deal where, if I would delay publication of the Hughes book for two years, Howard Hughes would give my author a face-to-face interview.

It was clear to me that Bautzer was playing a stalling game and I said: "Thanks, but no thanks."

The Hughes machine went into action. An attorney named Chester Davis set up a corporation called Rosemont Industries which claimed to own all rights in the life story of Howard Hughes. A secret deal was then made with Ezra Goodman. Goodman's contract with me provided that I couldn't change a comma of his script. His deal with Rosemont Industries gave them the right to edit any script before it was turned in to me.

For this Goodman received a check from Rosemont Industries for $42,750.

I'm a lucky fellow. I have friends in high places. One of them tipped me off to Ezra Goodman's secret deal, and I was able to smoke it out. I sued Goodman in arbitration and was awarded the return of the $10,000 advance I paid him. He then declared personal bankruptcy for more than $300,000. I was the only creditor who fought the issue.

Former FBI agent Norman Ollestad acted as my California attorney. In an unprecedented decision, a California judge denied Goodman's bankruptcy application. But before I could collect my $10,000, Ezra Goodman vanished. (He has since gone to the hell from whence he came.)

I contacted my Philadelphia attorney and good friend, Albert B. Gerber. I knew I could trust him not to be bought off the way Goodman had been. Gerber wrote an excellent Howard Hughes biography which I titled *Bashful Billionaire*, thus giving the shy hermit a new alias. I told my staff that if it made the best-seller list of *The New York Times*, I'd treat them all to a bonus vacation in Europe. It did and I did—all 38 of them. For 23 days they lived like millionaires London, Monte Carlo, Rome and Frankfurt.

· While we were in London, someone bought a copy of the international edition of *Time*. There, in the number one spot on *Time's* best-seller list was our *The Rich and the Super-Rich* by Ferdinand Lundberg. And back in New York, our warehouse was locked tight and for the next three weeks, frustrated booksellers and jobbers couldn't obtain additional copies of the book.

It was just after we returned from this pleasure-journey that I was called upon to appear before the Gaming Board in Carson City. Milton Prell warned me that there was a lot of static about my license, and it was all coming from the Hughes camp.

My Nevada attorney and I flew from Las Vegas to Reno. In the morning before our scheduled drive to Carson City, I dropped in to Harrah's.

A young man stood alone at the dice table shooting. He put a silver dollar on the line and picked up the dice. I decided to bet with him. He threw a long numbers-packed hand, but he never made his point. When he finally sevened out, I'd won $8,000 and he lost his dollar.

I tossed him a black ($100) chip and enjoyed the startled surprise and the delight on his face almost as much as my win. Then I joined my attorney for the charade that was to take place.

IN CARSON CITY, it was clear after a few minutes of strained double-talk that, as the old expression goes, "the fix was in." The buy-off was so obvious that some members of the Gaming Board appeared to be acting out a Three Stooges comedy script. It seems, they explained, that they were objecting to two titles in my mail-order catalog of 350 books that had been distributed by a subsidiary company of mine several years earlier.

Under questioning, the three Board members conceded that they hadn't actually seen the books and didn't know their content, but from their catalog descriptions, decided they must be "obscene."

I should point out that in my entire publishing career I have never had any trouble with the law on any level regarding the things I published. And these have included items like *The Sensuous Women* which started the Sexual Revolution and *The Anarchist Cookbook*, which tells how to blow up police stations and make Molotov cocktails.

The hearing room was small and occupied by only a handful of observers. These included a trio of Howard Hughes attorneys, all of whom sat in the back row smirking.

My attorney struggled to cope with the convoluted Board's reasoning on why it might be dangerous to grant a license to me. Even if the two titles they named weren't "dirty" (their word!) I *might* publish something naughty in the future!

Although another of my attorneys was once told that my FBI file is one of the largest in the Bureau's history (turn over in your grave, Al Capone!), in my entire adult life, no law enforcement agency has ever accused me of anything more serious than parking at a bus stop. Nobody was accusing the Board members of anything either, but one of the three felt it necessary to announce defensively that he hadn't been influenced by the Hughes people.

The farce was played out and I was turned down. I felt a mixture of amusement and anger—mostly anger. (We'll address ourselves further on to the foolishness of playing while you're upset.)

Five minutes later, without hearings of any kind, or meeting with him, even once, the commissioners granted Howard Hughes a license to own and operate the Desert Inn. It was his first Las Vegas casino. He hadn't even bothered to fill out or sign the application forms.

I drove to Lake Tahoe and lost the $8,000 I'd won in the morning plus a couple of thousand more. Then I drove to Reno and flew back to Las Vegas.

I was staying at The Sands, and when I walked into the casino I was approached by Charley Turner, one of the owners. He congratulated me on my "good fortune" in being turned down because "that joint [the Aladdin] can't make it."

Both Las Vegas newspapers were already headlining the turndown. The *Sun's* Hank Greenspun published a front page editorial condemning the Board because, he said, its decision against me would scare off other "respectable businessmen." Hank called the action "irresponsible" and concluded his column with the following:

Few of us, no matter what State we live in, are paragons of virtue and we recognize that Nevadans must be even more virtuous than residents of

States where gambling is not legal. But our image can suffer if the rest of the nation laughs at us.

THE NEXT DAY, also on the front page, Greenspun, in a full-length column, reminded the Board of errors the gaming control agency had made in the past. He cited the fact that it had turned down applications from generals in the U.S. Armed Forces. He added,

Frankly, sex shocks me once in a great while…. And I have been shocked by actions of past gaming control members who carried on shamefully with broads on the Strip. But that doesn't mean I would deny them the right to a livelihood because I don't admire their taste in women, or possibly caught them in a compromising situation.

NONE OF THIS softened my anger. That evening, shortly after my return to Las Vegas, I drove to the Aladdin. Within a short time I signed $18,000 worth of markers at the dice pit. Then I seated myself at the baccarat table. There were three shills ("starters") and one real player who faced me from the other end of the table.

The limit was $2,000 a hand, and I was betting the limit. Soon I was $10,000 "on the rim." That made a total of $28,000 I owed the Aladdin.

Prell's brother-in-law, casino manager Gil Gilbert, stood observing the game. "Gil," I said, "give me another $12,000. That'll make an even forty. But if you give me any more, I won't pay it."

If you give me any more, I won't pay it. Those are the powerful words—especially effective where a casino is eager to "stretch and break" you.

Within the next ten minutes, I lost another $10,000.

On two hands, the fellow playing at the opposite end of the table beat me by such close scores as 5 to 4 and 6 to 5. He was playing $20 a hand while I was playing $2,000.

"Great," I remarked after one such close defeat.

"I don't feel so good winning my small bet when I see how much you're losing," he said. (A kind remark, considering that most gamblers are rightfully "I'm-for-me-first" players.)

I was down to my last $2,000 as the shoe was passed to the fellow at the opposite end.

Instead of betting the usual $2,000—I decided to prolong the ordeal. It was around 10 P.M. After I lost this two grand, I'd have lots of time to kill, since I'd now cut off credit. Feeling as I did, I had no desire to see a show, have sex, or walk in the desert. Instead of $2,000, I placed three hundred dollars* in the Player box

"Why don't you go with me just once?" the man called to me from across the table.

"Why? Are you going to do good?"

"I'm going to make four passes!"

He had been betting on Bank and I had consistently bet against him on Player. What the hell, I thought. What's another ten minutes? I picked up the three hundred-dol-

---

*In those days, baccarat was played with cash. Newcomers who are amazed to hear this are even more amazed to learn that, in those days, the players helped shuffle the cards!

lar bills and pushed these and my remaining $1,700 onto the Bank side.

He made one pass. A second. A third. Then he dealt a tie.

"Nothing personal!" I said as I followed a belly hunch and pulled the money over to the Player side. Player won.

Within a few minutes, he and I were laughing it up— calling to each other, "What are you gonna do now?" and playing on the same side.

Having observed what was happening, Gil Gilbert became upset. He leaned over and whispered something into the man's ear. I jumped up and raced over to the other side of the table.

"What's the matter?" I demanded.

"Nothing, Lyle. I just thought this gentleman was bothering you," Gil said, as he lamely retreated.

"Bothering me?" I replied. "Next to my wife and kids, this nice man is the best friend I have in the world! *Don't bother him!*"

When the shoe had been dealt out, I decided to cash in.

"Gil, I have an $18,000 marker in the dice pit. Would you get it for me, please?"

I counted my cash. I had won back all my losses and was now $5,600 ahead. One remark from a stranger had altered my play and resulted in a turnaround of more than $80,000 in less than fifteen minutes.

When I finished counting my money, and looked up to thank the stranger, he had vanished.

We met again in the same casino several months later. "What happened to you that night?" I asked. "You disappeared on me! I couldn't even buy you dinner or a drink!"

"Aw," he said graciously, "I could see you were busy so I didn't want to hang around and bother you."

9

THAT FICKLE FINGER

Y ou've heard these tag lines:

"Remember, the more you bet, the less you lose when you win."

"The O of the O." (The opposite of the obvious.)

"Don't say you didn't win—say you didn't play!"

ALL WHO'VE GAMBLED in casinos over an extended period of time can boast of some very happy experiences. And, of course, some memorably miserable ones.

There was a time when I was a regular visitor and winner at a now-defunct London casino called A Pair of Shoes. Dapper dope-smoking Eric Steiner liked to call his elegant Edwardian, plush-lined gilt-and-crystal emporium "a small social club." He fronted the place. Even today I doubt that many know who the identity of the real owners.

A Pair of Shoes was an "in" place for celebrities. On this night, *Time-Life* magazine publisher Henry Luce and his wife Clare were in the dining room. Actors Geraldine and Sydney Chaplin were upstairs in the intimate casino.

TV talk-show host David Susskind sat on a plush sofa surrounded by three beautiful young damsels.

Eric Steiner decided to show off.

"You're a sport," Steiner said, as he greeted me when I walked in with a group of guests. "I'll bet you $1,000 on one hand of dice."

That was about ten times the table max on wagers. I accepted his challenge, but I wouldn't agree to bet with the player then throwing the dice, or with Bill Cosby, the next shooter. Steiner, on the other hand, didn't want me to be the shooter. Nor would I agree to let him shoot. We finally decided on my British cousin, who was in a casino for the first time in her life.

She tossed the dice. A 2 and a 1. Craps. A loser. I handed Steiner a thousand-dollar bill.

(My cousin later explained that she thought the goal of the game was to get those little dice cubes as close to the other end of the table as possible!)

I wandered over to the blackjack tables. Within minutes I won back the thousand and then some.

Steiner was upset when he saw me at the cage cashing in my chips.

"Lyle, from now on, use this place as your private club. Be our guest for dinner and drinks. But do your playing elsewhere. You're too lucky for us."

It took me a moment to realize he was in dead earnest. I was flattered.

The next night was our last in London. My first wife, Mary Louise, and I went to the Playboy Club. Its dice table had a £50 limit (about $75) and I placed max-limit bets on the inside numbers (5, 6, 8, and 9) and quickly lost two thousand dollars. The casino was thick with people and thicker with the cigarette smoke that both Mary Louise and I detested. (The building was originally built as executive offices for an appliance distributor, and the ventilation system for the narrow floor was designed to ventilate an area occupied by thirty people rather than three hundred.)

Mary Louise, who rarely complained, now suggested that we go elsewhere. And I, who was rarely cross with her, said with expressed irritation, "Look, I want to stay here a while! Do me a favor and play some blackjack."

My tone was angry and I felt guilty as she turned without a word and walked toward the blackjack tables, whose female dealers were all dressed in Playboy's scanty bunny costumes.

I plunged back into the craps game.

For a short time, I won and I lost. There was no trend as the dice moved around the crowded table. Then it was my turn again to shoot and I was about to have one of those mystical experiences that are every dice player's dream.

I threw number after number after number. I made pass after pass after pass. The chips piled up in front of me—for I had all the numbers covered by come bets and topped with maximum odds money.

Craps is a primitive game and in an American casino is quick and volatile. Anywhere out of the U.S.A. it is often a relatively slow game. There are interminable delays in the action because dealers aren't skilled in quick and proper payoffs. Thus it was that in the middle of my great shoot, a stranger tapped me on the arm and said, "Did you hear about the player at Caesars Palace who held the dice for half an hour?"

I had indeed. But that wasn't the point. As every dice player knows, there are certain widely held superstitions about the game of craps: If a die jumps off the table, the next roll inevitably will be "out-7." If a die hits somebody's hand, the dice will 7-out. If a wife says to her husband, "How are you doing?" his next roll will 7-out.

It's nonsense of course, but, as with religious belief, it has a large following.

My next roll was *not* a 7-out. I was pleased that the man's conversation didn't bother me. I continued to roll and roll and roll. Meanwhile, I kept looking around, trying to locate my wife through the smoky room. I felt vindicated by my decision to stay on and I wanted her to enjoy the fact that I was doing so well. No sign of her.

I started to show off. I tossed the dice backwards. Under my arm. Over my shoulder. I bounced them. I tossed them high in the air. I could do no wrong.

Finally I became concerned. I wanted to make contact with my wife.

"I pass," I announced, after making another point.

There was a loud chorus of "No!" and "Don't" and "Please, don't!"

With a sign of resignation, I picked the cubes up again, and continued to throw them onto the green felt table. Finally, when I was coming out for a new point, I announced: "I know how I'll get out of here! My odds are working!"

(It's a house rule that the odds placed on "come" bets don't work on the first or come-out roll unless the player says otherwise. Thus, if the shooter throws a 7, his odds money is returned to him even though the casino wins the "come" bets.)

I threw a 7.

Silently, the dealers picked up the line bets from fifteen players. They took my place money and my odds money. The entire jam-packed ring of people around the table stood transfixed. Mesmerized. An oil painting.

Only when the stickman started to push the dice to the shooter to my left did somebody come out of the group trance to shout, "Wait a minute! He *won!* He rolled a 7!"

Pandemonium. Supervisors were rushed over to guide the dealers in their crisis.

Each player was asked the amount of his wager. The bet was reconstituted and then paid off. Again and again, a dealer would say, "But, sir, you were only betting one pound, not ten—" and a casino executive would cut him off with, "Pay him. Put ten pounds on the line and pay him another ten. This was our mistake."

The dice were mine again. I continued to throw them for at least another ten minutes. When finally I sevened out, the tuxedo-clad gentleman in charge announced: "Ladies and gentlemen, this table will be closed for a short time."

There was a chorus of moans, groans and protests. Through the smoke-filled room I suddenly spotted Mary Louise at a distant blackjack table. (I later learned that she won a neat $800, and this was gambling with minimum bets.)

I was in a hurry to share the good news with my wife, but first the casino supplied seversal racks into which I stacked my newly won chips. The man in the tuxedo helped me carry them to the cashier's cage.

"Why did you close the table? Were my dice too lucky?"

"No," he said. "But you've cleaned out the cage." He smiled. "You've literally broken the bank."

I thought he was jesting but he wasn't. I was asked to accept all kinds of European currency as well as all kinds of money orders. The cashier was still short $2,600. A Playboy check for that amount was written on a London bank to my order.

I returned to New York City the next day. In the usual course of things, I deposited the Playboy check.

Weeks later, I happened to remember that I hadn't received a notice of its having cleared. I asked Carlos Gonzalez, the comptroller of my book publishing company, to call the bank and make inquiry. The bank told him that the Bank of England was being unusually slow in clearing checks.

Two days later, England devalued the pound by 10 percent.

I wrote to the Playboy Club with a copy of my bank clearance slip. I had lost $260 in the devaluation and pointed out that it wasn't my fault that Playboy's cashier cage didn't have funds enough to pay me fully in cash.

At that time, the London Playboy Club was run by Victor Lownes, and under his direction had become the most profitable casino in the world. The Playboy people were good about it. Back came an airmail note of apology with a check for $260, drawn on an American bank.

The Playboy Club experience had been another lucky one. But I was an average "high roller" who won and lost large amounts and knew what it was all about only slightly more than most "low rollers."

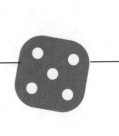

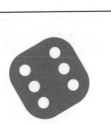

10

THE COMPULSIVE GAMBLER

I'm tempted to begin any discussion of gambling with a
sermon against it. All gamblers are fools, myself included. Any gambling that risks your losing enough money to
affect your standard of living or add to your worries is self-
destructive. The best gamble is not to gamble at all. I
would then add that if you accept this premise, but are
going to gamble anyway, this book could be helpful.

I don't happen to be a compulsive gambler. Compulsive
gambling is a very serious disease. I have watched a man
gamble away his entire lingerie business in one evening. I
have known another who couldn't face his gambling debts
and killed himself. For those with the disease, I strongly
recommend a phone call to Gamblers Anonymous.

In Atlantic City, casinos are required to warn the players, "Bet with your head, not over it." They don't mean it,
anymore than the cigarette companies mean it when they
carry those law-mandated warnings on cigarette packs and
in cigarette ads that tell you how you shorten your life and
destroy yourself when you smoke.

Allow me to keep reminding you that casino gambling is nothing more than entertainment. Casinos may offer good entertainment, lavish entertainment, exciting entertainment but the bottom line is: it's expensive entertainment.

Recently, Emmy nominee Gail O'Grady of the TV series *NYPD Blue* was reported by a weekly tabloid to have lost so many hundreds of thousands of dollars to high-stakes slot machines, that she was evicted from her Hollywood mansion and forced to move into a converted toolshed the size of a double garage behind the home of her former manager.

The 31-year-old sexy and beautiful blonde lost thousands of dollars an hour. She went through a $470,000 divorce settlement. In her bankruptcy papers, she listed casinos to whom she owed money. They were Caesars Palace, $88,000; Bally's Casino, $21,494; and the Tropicana, $7,500.

Her unfortunate compulsion has been widely publicized because of her show business celebrity. But there are similar tragedies among hundreds of people less widely known.

IN JUNE, 1994, Carole and I attended the *9th International Conference on Gambling & Risk-Taking*. This was held at the MGM Grand in Las Vegas. It was sponsored and organized by the Institute of Gambling and Commercial Gaming at the College of Business Administration of the University of Nevada in Reno.

We'd attended a previous conference many years ago in Lake Tahoe.

Two things struck me as being very different about this one. First, it had a truly international flavor. Men and women were there from Spain, the United Kingdom, Australia, Denmark and Portugal.

Secondly, and of greater import, was that of the 180 separate papers read on every conceivable gaming-related topic, at least 55 were on the subject of the problem gambler and compulsive gambling.

Compulsive Gambling was recognized officially as a mental disease by the American Psychiatric Association in 1980.

We heard some startling stories. There was, for example, a report from a farmer. He said, "I love my wife. I love her dearly. She has worked very hard on the farm with me."

His wife toiled long and hard, side-by-side with him to make a success of their farm. She gave birth to three children and even while caring for them, worked sunrise to sunset in the fields.

One day she told her husband she was going to play bingo on the following evening. He was pleased. At last she would be able to get away and have time for herself.

Soon she was playing bingo twice a week. Then, for an entire year, she played bingo every night of the week. Her husband didn't learn the full extent of her compulsion until he was notified that their farm was to be foreclosed and that she had pawned her wedding ring.

OR, THERE WAS the woman who reported: "I have to sleep with my pocketbook under my pillow because my 16-year-old son steals from me in order to feed his gambling addiction."

COMPULSIVE GAMBLERS usually feel compelled to lose. They plan to play with a set amount of money and for a certain time. They always lose and leave the casino only to get more funds to do more gambling. They're stopped only by exhaustion, sickness, legal intervention or suicide. (Las Vegas is the suicide capital of America.)

Casinos don't need this. The president of Foxwoods recently observed that a single story in the news about a person who lost his or her college tuition or house or automobile in a casino will cost more than the casino could have won from that player. The price of overcoming the negative impression in a marketing campaign is tremendous.

Those Indian tribes in Minnesota know the pain of compulsions from observing their brothers and sisters addicted to alcohol. To its credit, the Minnesota Indian Gaming Association was quick to organize a program under the Minnesota Counsel on Casino Gambling. Under it, all 12,000 employees of the Indian casinos in that State were trained to look for and recognize the danger systems of problem behavior. They were taught to encourage the compulsive gambler to get help.

The forces of temptation and persuasion are overwhelming. In Minnesota, for example, the State spends nearly eight million dollars a year in advertising its lottery.

New York mental hygiene experts estimate that 1.5 percent of our total population or about 2,800,000 men and women are pathological gamblers.

ARE YOU COMPULSIVE? Is gambling an addiction for you? I hope not. This book is written for people who genuinely want to win.

11

GAMBLING INTERMISSION

FOR ME

I go to the racetrack once a year, if that often. I do it as a social thing. Gambling on horses* bores me. So do baseball and football betting.

I don't gamble in any of the Islands (people who gamble in Puerto Rico casinos are compulsive losers), and I no longer gamble in London or anywhere in Europe because I want to play only where I can walk from casino to casino.

Months have gone by when I didn't have time to visit a casino. I didn't give it a second thought. Nor have I ever lost more money than I could comfortably afford to lose— that is, than I could pay without affecting the living standards of my family.

In 1969, my first wife, Mary Louise, died of cancer. She died in my arms in a house in Port Maria, Jamaica. She died without taking a painkiller because she wanted to be con-

---

*I don't like to bet on anything that breathes but can't talk back to me to explain why it didn't do what it was supposed to do. Nick the Greek went one step further. He said he wouldn't bet on anything that eats.

scious of her family to her dying breath. Local doctors could never understand how she endured the pain.

After that, for a long time, I didn't care about anything. When I went to casinos I lost large amounts of money. Shortly before her death, I received an unexpected check for $498,000 from the sale of stock. The money couldn't help her survive so it meant nothing to me.

A pattern was set. There were times when I won, but more often I lost. Either way didn't seem to matter. My playing was listless and drugged. I didn't give it much thought. One year after her death, I took twenty-four members of my publishing staff on a bonus vacation to Los Angeles and San Francisco. Our final destination was Las Vegas where four hotels gave me three suites each, and all of my staff were comped for their rooms and all they could eat and drink.

While some of my young men from the shipping room were waking up to champagne and breakfast steaks, I had become an unwilling tour director and by the time we all left town, I had, in my lethargy, dropped $140,000.

A few weeks later, *Life* magazine was researching a feature article about me and asked that I go back to Las Vegas so I could be photographed in the casinos. I dutifully did. Of the 15 or so photographs that were published to illustrate the article, only two came from that visit. On which occasion I dropped another $60,000— making a $200,000 loss in two months. I had no feelings about any of it.

Time passed and the listless losing pattern continued. Then I got lucky again. A lady named Carole Livingston became my frequent companion. In 1982, she became my wife.

One day Carole and I were guests at Caesars Palace for the Alan King Tennis Classic (I still don't know where the tennis courts are) which was a celebrity-studded affair. It seemed that every other face you saw was someone you recognized from your television or movie screens. But the super-star was obviously Sidney Poitier—for while people stared at and pointed to the other celebrities, they grouped around Poitier as though he were the Pied Piper.

I avoided Poitier. He and I had been in the same weekly poker game for many years and occasionally we'd lunched together. He'd known Mary Louise and when she became ill I thought he could have sent her a get-well card or made an encouraging phone call. Nothing.

When news of her death appeared in *The New York Times,* he twice called the office of a mutual friend, Broadway producer Philip Rose. He asked Phil for my home phone number, but he didn't call me, and I hadn't heard from him.

So whenever I saw him in the casino, I detoured to avoid a confrontation.

At about 2:30 A.M., Carole and I were attracted by a huge crowd surrounding a blackjack table at Caesars Palace. Curious, we joined the crowd. Sidney was sitting with Diana Ross, who was headlining the Caesars show.

"Let's move closer," Carole said. "I want to see what he looks like."

"You know what he looks like," I said, irritated. Sidney had, in fact, visited our offices in Manhattan and patiently posed for an individual Polaroid picture with each of the forty members of our staff.

We stood at the back edge of the two hundred or so who comprised the crowd. Sidney swung around on his stool, surveying the darkened casino. He wore the glazed look of the celebrity who has been stared at long and hard.

Suddenly he did a double-take and swung around again.

"Lyle!" he called out, jumping up. The crowd parted to allow him through as he came toward me. I held out my hand stiffly and said a cold "Hello, Sidney." He pushed my hand aside and embraced me.

In the course of conversation, he asked about my children. (You can't be angry with someone who inquires about your children.)

I asked how he was doing.

"What do you mean?"

"At the tables. Here."

"I don't gamble anymore."

"What do you mean, you don't gamble? What about Phil Rose's poker game?"

"I haven't been in the game for nearly two years."*

"Why?"

The words he then spoke couldn't have taken more than two minutes to say. I often wish that I had taped them. He made the point that when you give money to a casino, you diminish your family and everything for which you've worked. He also made the point that if you had sur-

---

*Sidney told me that to convince himself that he was free of the gambling bug, he'd bought $10,000 worth of white and yellow chips ($500 and $1,000 denominations), filled his pockets with them and wandered through the casino for an entire day without making a bet.

plus money to disburse, you could better spend it on food for the hungry people of the world. But this summary really doesn't do justice to what he said.

Even as he talked, I recognized the truth in what he was saying.

I joked that it was too bad he hadn't talked to me $59,000 sooner. I promised to try to catch up with him when he played tennis at 10 o'clock that morning, but at 10 A.M. Carole and I were in our rented car—having decided to leave town.

We started our drive to McCarran Airport (named after one of the most ruthless and honest United States Senators in history). I suddenly turned left and pulled into the driveway of the Aladdin. The valet took the car, and as we approached the entrance doors I remarked to Carole, "This is an historic moment."

She had no idea what I meant.

I'd decided to give up gambling for a while. Sidney Poitier's 120-second sermon had given me a fresh perspective.

I'd stopped off at the Aladdin because up to that time and from the day I had become a temporary point owner, I had never lost money at the tables of that particular casino.

We only had a few minutes to spare but in those few minutes I won more than $5,000, thus reducing my net loss for the visit to $54,000.

On the further drive to the airport, I mentioned to Carole that I believed I wouldn't be gambling again for a while. I wasn't giving it up forever, but what Sidney said made sense to me. He had talked about gambling in a context that I'd never before considered.

For the next two years I didn't make a wager of any kind. Not even to the extent of buying a lottery* ticket.

---

*One of the worst wagers you can make, to be sure. Worse than any wager available in the casino, for the State immediately takes 50 percent as a tax. Nevertheless, the year before I'd needed change for a parking meter and to get it, I bought four 50-cent lottery tickets for my daughter, Sandy, and she won $5,000 on one of the tickets.

12

I RETURN TO THE TABLES

Early on, I mentioned my ten consecutive winning visits to Las Vegas. Contrary to what one not-too-savvy book reviewer wrote, they weren't "pure luck." Of course I had been lucky. Nor did I do any of the winning dishonestly or with any edge except a reasonably rigid adherence to a combination of the wisdoms I am going to impart to you in the pages that follow.

But, first, let me share with you my thoughts prior to those ten visits.

As I told you, I'd decided to absent myself from casino gambling for a while. I would, nevertheless from time-to-time, consider resuming gambling.

One observation that stuck with me was that during the years of my first marriage I had won sometimes and I had lost sometimes. But Mary Louise, playing with small amounts of money, had come away winners fourteen out of sixteen times.

Fourteen out of sixteen times! What was *her* secret?

For one thing, she knew the rules of the games she played (blackjack and craps). She had an interesting philosophy. She believed that in almost every combat with the casino there is a point during which the player is ahead. That's the point at which you quit.

You quit winners!

Moreover, if anything bothered her at a table—the attitude of another player —a remark by a dealer —the smoke from a cigarette or cigar—she would get up and walk away. Promptly. Without hesitation. For she believed that one had to be in an affirmative mood if one was to make correct decisions and properly manage one's money. Any irritation could work to one's detriment.*

Some of what I'll say in these pages may disturb you. Some of it may clash head-on with your own deeply held beliefs. It has only one thing going for it: two decades ago, it worked ten times in a row. And today, when I apply it, it works again and again.

I've known many people who gamble regularly. I have never known any of them to win ten times in a row. These people include Mannie Kimmel, who is "Mister X" in

---

*Mario Puzo, on reading the manuscript of my first gaming book, told me I was being hard on smokers. The fact is that, fair or not, I judge people by whether they smoke cigarettes. I consider cigarette smokers to be born losers. They're losers on many levels in life. Cigarette smokers live an average of three years less than nonsmokers. The Surgeon General has pointed out that 30 percent of all deaths from cancer can be attributed to cigarettes.

Kissing a woman who smokes cigarettes is like kissing a dirty ashtray. In my bachelor days, I never made a second date with any woman who smoked cigarettes.

End of sermon. If you smoke, the time to quit is now. Not January. Not next Monday. Not tomorrow morning. Now. This minute!

I hate to leave a casino smelling of your cigarette smoke!

books by Thorp and John Scarne, and who is said to have once lost half a million dollars to Nick the Greek on a single bet on a presidential election. They include shift bosses, supervisors, pit bosses and dealers and casino owners. Not one of them has been able to tell me of anyone who wins that consistently.

Think about that. Then pay special heed to the guidance that follows.

Sometimes, to make you get the point, I'll repeat myself quite deliberately. And some of what I tell you will seem paradoxical and have its own built-in contradictions. But all told, what you are about to read is razor-sharp and guru-true.

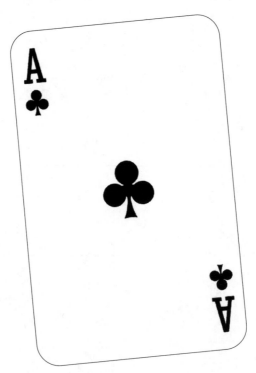

13

THE BABE RUTH FORMULA:

HIT-AND-RUN

The primary thing you must understand if you are to become a steady winner is that *The contest is not between you and the casino. It is between you and yourself.*

Winning in a casino is a combination of self-discipline and luck. If you are savvy, you know what to do. (Or you can learn.) But unless you are disciplined, you won't do it, and in time you will lose.

You must set your own rules—*and follow them.* To the extent that you do, you will win. To the extent that you don't, you will inevitably pay the piper.

Only you can make the decision on whether you want to play to play, or play to win.

Rule 1: Hit-and-run. The casinos will hate you for it, but IT IS THE ONLY WAY YOU CAN CONSISTENTLY WALK AWAY WITH THEIR MONEY.

In almost every game you play, there will most likely be a time when you are ahead. Put aside a part of those winnings with your original stake, so that no matter what happens from then on, YOU MUST LEAVE THE TABLE A WINNER.

You can never go wrong walking away with a profit. Never worry about what you "might have won" if you lingered longer!

Failure to follow this strategy is why most people are losers in casinos.

WHEN I VIOLATE my rule against taking friends with me, I sometimes make use of them to enforce a little discipline trick that works well for me. If, for example, my wife Carole is standing behind me, and I've won several hands at blackjack or craps or baccarat, I'll turn to her and say, "The first hand I lose, I leave."

I've now made a public announcement. I'm committed. And when I lose a hand, I feel obligated to quit. Carole is my lucky charm and my enforcer: it has worked time and time again.

I remembered to include this only after the first draft of this book was written. I was lunching with two friends. Dan Simon and John Oakes. They run a small but classy publishing house called *Four Walls Eight Windows*.

They reminded me of what we'd done for each other in the gaming arena.

One day, shortly before Christmas, they were a little under the weather because of disappointing sales on some of their titles. Dan and John had assisted us in editing some of our successful books including *Living the Martial Way* by Major Forrest E. Morgan and *The Encyclopedia of Unusual Sex Practices* by Brenda Love. I decided to thank them and maybe lift their spirits by taking them to Atlantic City.

We talked book publishing in the limousine. But after we arrived in A.C. we never mentioned books again. They both were impressed by the reception, penthouse and royal treatment I received.

The first thing I did in the casino was to open a baccarat game. I told them we'd play a few hands. John Oakes cut the cards. His cut was a good cut for him, disaster for me. I gave them each some chips and instructed them to bet against me. They did. Betting against me, and following my instructions on how much to wager each time, they each won about $2,500. At the same time, in twelve hands I dropped $34,000.

We left the table.

"Your winnings are what you go home with," I declared. "I might treat you to a little action at the slot machines but no more real gambling for either of you!"

They were shocked by the size of my loss, and puzzled because I seemed unaffected and in such good spirits. I assured them that I had come to the casino to win some money and win some money I would. They were unconvinced. From the way they looked at each other, I believe they thought I was a little crazy.

An hour later, they watched while I sat at a blackjack table playing three hands at $3,000 each. Their mouths hung open as I won round after round. Back to me came the $34,000 I'd dropped at baccarat. And I continued to win more hands than I lost. I was running lucky.

Then I lost a complete round. Three hands. $9,000.

I didn't want to give back everything I'd won. I used my faithful gimmick.

"Okay fellows," I announced to them and everyone else

within hearing distance, "The next hand I lose, I leave."

On the next round I won one, lost one and tied one.

"That's it!" John and Dan said in chorus.

I was reluctant to quit. I tried to rationalize. "Yeah, but the hand I lost was canceled by the hand I won."

They didn't buy it. "No! No" they said, each one taking one of my arms. "You've got to leave. You're supposed to be a man of your word!"

They were right and I was wrong and I knew it. I got up to leave the table and they lifted me bodily from my stool.

We had a gourmet lunch. We played some slot machines. Then I called for the limousine to take us home. In the limo, I counted my money. I was a $27,000 winner. John and Dan had each won nearly $2,800. (Plus my gratitude for insisting that I keep my word and quit when I lost that hand.)

A simple gimmick, but it works for me.

And you don't need company. If you're on a winning streak, don't be seduced by greed. Tell yourself you'll stop playing after you lose a hand. Then do so.

THE IMPORTANCE of what you have just read can't be stressed too strongly. There is no way you can play any casino game over an extended time and come away a winner. Percentage will grind you out. Losing streaks will destroy all of your elaborate plans and systems.

Studies show that women are better able to this than are men. With men, there seems to be a self-esteem problem. Ego gets in the way of wisdom and so men play on, losing back what they've won—and then are driven by pride to try to recoup.

Women are not as ego-involved and are much better able to walk away winners and leave the ego-feeding for the lollipop.

NOT PLAYING long enough to let the percentage chew you up is the reason that some casinos won't pay air fare for a player unless the player stays three nights. (If you don't lose your bankroll in three nights, you aren't really trying!)

Where lesser comps are involved, the casino insists on three or four hours of play a day, and with $25 chips.

The job of the people who run those abattoir-efficient casinos is to keep you playing until you lose your stake.

Your job is to play until you have some of their money—and then beat a happy retreat to the nearest exit.

14

LEARNING THE SCORE

I n Las Vegas there is a splendid book shop known as the Gamblers Book Club. It issues quarterly bulletins and offers the most extensive collection of gaming books in the world. Read everything you can on the game or games of your choice. Knowledge is win-power.

It was founded in 1964 by the late John Luckman, whom I first knew as a blackjack dealer at Caesars Palace. It is owned by his widow Edna and operates under the brilliant direction of marketing director and store manager Howard Schwartz. It's a meeting place for people interested in gambling. There is no other book shop like it in the world. It's worth taking time out for a visit every time you're in Vegas. Their free 32-page catalog listing more than 1,000 different titles can be yours for a phone call to 1-800-522-1777. Or write for a catalog to GBC, 630 South 11th Street, Las Vegas, NV 89101. The catalog will be mailed to you first class.

There was a newsletter called *Rouge & Noir*. There was a high-priced newsletter called *The High Roller* which

I published with Paul Schumer, a close friend. (It was successful but I became bored with it.) There was a magazine published by Stanley Sludikoff called *Gambling Times* which was succeeded by a magazine called *Win*. All have 7nd-out. (The offices of *Win* were destroyed by the California earthquake. Publication has been suspended for half-a-year although its staff says it will come to life again.)

Currently, *Casino Player* is a magazine chock full of information, casino ads, and advice to players. A one-year subscription is $24, and in addition to the twelve monthly issues, you'll receive bonus gifts in the way of casino coin vouchers and coupons. Its address is 2524 Arctic Avenue, Atlantic City, NJ 08401.

There are other more serious periodicals for blackjack professionals. *Blackjack Forum* is a quarterly published by Arnold Snyder. *Current Blackjack News* is published monthly by Stanford Wong. These are exceptional because they tell serious players of rules changes, bonus moves in promotions, suspected cheating and which casinos turn the most "heat" on suspected counters.

Of those other expensive newsletters that float around, I can only say that if their writers really had a handle on gaming, they'd be at the casino tables instead of at their computers.

Tools of knowledge can't hurt and sometimes they help. But please dwell on this next sentence:

THERE ARE NO SYSTEMS

There are approaches. There are good wagers and bad wagers. There are money management tricks. There is intuition. There is luck. *But there are no systems that will defeat any casino table game over a period of time.*

Michael Konik, gambling columnist for *Cigar Aficionado* recently commented: "Foolproof betting systems, alas, are primarily utilized by fools."

If you can't accept this, you're a dreamer or a fool or both. The more you're willing to wager on your system, the more readily will the casino send one of its limousines for you.

In early June, 1994, a very rich and foolish dreamer in Indonesia was convinced he had a system to beat baccarat. The new billion-dollar MGM Grand in Las Vegas dispatched a private plane for him. His wagers were as high as $100,000 a hand. He played in a private salon, cut off from public view by a velvet curtain. He played for 24 hours without a break. Then he quit for some sleep. He awoke and resumed play. The next day when he flew home, he had lost $2,200,000.

He probably still believes he can beat baccarat.

IF YOU SEEK a sure-fire system, you are Jason in search of the Golden Fleece. And it's you who is ripe for the fleecing.

There *are* gaming approaches and attitudes. The only "system" I know after a lifetime of gambling is a combination of the rules and attitudes that I offer you in this book. If you think otherwise, you're a True Believer and a natural victim.

IN MY FIRST BOOK, I said much of what you've just read. This infuriated publisher Stanley Sludikoff, who taught blackjack under the pseudonym of Stanley Roberts and who published a wide variety of gambling books and the one-time above-mentioned monthly magazine, *Gambling Times*.

As most gaming magazines do, *Gambling Times* depended on advertisers. And since casinos were not then educated to the value of such ads, most of the *Gambling Times* revenue came from people selling systems by mail. So, when Stanley Sludikoff reviewed *Casino Gambling for the Winner* his review was a diatribe that included the statement that my book was a fraud.

I sued for libel. While the suit was pending, I entered a baccarat tournament at an Atlantic City hotel. I should have taken first place, but I blew it and came in second. (I describe the circumstances later.) When it was over and I stood up, Sludikoff stepped into the baccarat pit and introduced himself to me.

He commiserated with me on my dumb move. Then our talk turned to his attack on my integrity in his book review and he insisted that it had been fair and accurate.

The two of us strolled through the casino. Stanley watched while I won $32,000 at craps and another $11,000 at blackjack.

In those first twenty minutes, other strangers greeted me. Two men told me how helpful my book had been to them.

A woman approached me. "Mr. Stuart, I don't know how to thank you! Last month my husband won $6,000 *and he came home with it.* This never happened before and it was all because of your book!"

Sludikoff blanched slightly.

Minutes later, a young man stopped me. "You can't imagine how your book has changed my approach to gambling," he said. "Especially your Rule of Three."

I laughed. "I'll bet you'd believe these people were shills if I could have had any advance notice that I'd be meeting you!"

Sludikoff just grunted.

I added, "I'm going to destroy you in court. I've never lost a lawsuit in my life."

"Can this be settled?" he asked.

"Anything can be settled," I said.

We retired to the hotel's coffee shop where, over a bagel and cream cheese, I agreed to accept an apology, and $12,500 in free ads in *Gambling Times* magazine.

Stanley subsequently wrote in his magazine, "I found Lyle to be a warm and generous human being. When he met a young man who had obviously lost a sum of money which he apparently could not afford, I saw Lyle give this fellow enough money to help him out of a serious dilemma. To the best of my knowledge, that person had been a perfect stranger who recognized Lyle from the photograph on his book jacket . . . ."*

So it was settled. Except that Stanley's attorney neglected to withdraw a motion he'd made, and a judge ruled in his favor! Stanley won, but he'd already lost! This is what is known as "the luck factor." In this situation, I had it and Stanley didn't.

---

*I wore a beard then, which I've since shaved off. It caused too many to recognize me and tended to make me want to grandstand.

15

THE BEGINNING

OF WINNING

Time out to review my first three Commandments, and to look at a fourth.

1. Self-discipline
2. Quit when you're ahead
3. There are no systems

Get em? Got em? Good!

LET ME TELL you about Louis Holloway. Holloway was a delightful elderly fellow who lived in Las Vegas and earned his living gambling. He did it for thirty-five years. He wrote a book called *Full-Time Gambler* which I published but which is now out-of-print.

Holloway had a son who graduated MIT and was reputed to be a mathematics genius. "Dad," said the son one day, "you can't beat a casino. You can't overcome the odds. You just can't."

Holloway told me he replied, "You're right, son. You're absolutely right." He paused. "By the way, this house we're sitting in? That new automobile outside? That hefty college tuition I paid for you for four years? They all came from casino winnings. But you're absolutely right."

HOLLOWAY WAS a professional gambler. On several occasions, I made the rounds with him. I watched him win at blackjack. I watched him win at dice. Until a heart condition limited his activity, he played each day for an hour to an hour and a half. He won $40 to $75* every day. Then he quit. He played seven days a week. He spent other hours reading every new piece of literature to come out on every phase of gaming. He analyzed and discarded every system "guaranteed" to win.

Holloway was a counter at blackjack when the casinos dealt from one or two decks. He looked like a Presbyterian minister and no one paid attention to his modest play. His bets were $5 and $10. He exemplified our next rule of the game.

DON'T BE GREEDY.

Greed is a major ally of the casino. It stops you from following the QUIT WHEN YOU'RE A WINNER rule because when you're running good, you don't want their cash alone; you want the chandeliers, too.**

Greed is a natural enemy of self-discipline. It's a disease that causes you to lose perspective. You know that over any long period of time, the casino will defeat you.

---

*With inflation, we're talking $125 to $240 in today's dollars.
**Don't mistake the impact of this advice. Too many casino patrons let losses run up but limit their winnings. A casino shift boss once remarked about someone I know: "He's dangerous because he presses when he wins, and if you're not careful, he'll write you a new address!"

And yet you sit there or stand there unwilling to walk away with a big score because you're hungry for an even bigger one.

Let me cite two examples that I know first hand. A busboy at the New Frontier on the Strip went to gamble in a casino on downtown Fremont Street where a friend was dealing blackjack. The busboy had exactly $16 in his pocket. He sat at his friend's table and began to play.

This was no setup. In fact the dealer quickly told the pit boss that he knew the player and asked if it was okay to deal to him. He was told it was. The busboy got lucky. He went from blackjack to dice. He moved from the Mint to the Nugget and then on to the Horseshoe.

By 2 A.M. he had won more than $9,000.

He taxied back to his room near the Strip hotel where he worked. $9,000! He couldn't sleep. An hour later he was back on Fremont Street. By sunrise he had lost it all.

Arnold Levy is associated with my book publishing business. Years ago, he got very lucky in Las Vegas. He won $54,000. He and his companion went up to their room with the packets of $1,000, $500 and $100 bills. His companion pleaded with him to get a cashier's check or to put some in safekeeping. He told her not to worry. He stashed it all under his pillow.

If a pea kept a fairy tale princess from sleeping, try to imagine what $54,000 did to Arnold Bruce Levy. He couldn't sleep a wink. He was as restless as a jitterbug.

"Please, don't," his lady friend pleaded when he got out of bed and began to dress.

"Hell's bells!" he announced. "I'd be crazy to quit now when I'm on this great streak! I'm going downstairs and *double* it!"

When the couple returned to New York's Kennedy Airport the next day, his lady had to lay out cab fare to Manhattan.

If you know gamblers, you know lots of stories like these.

Here's rule #4 again:

DON'T BE GREEDY.

Two postscripts about my friend, Arnold. On one occasion he believed he had a sure-fire system. He would stand at a craps table, wait for the shooter to come out with a point and then place bets of $1,000 on the 5 and 9, $1,200 each on the 6 and 8 and he'd buy the 4 and 10 for $1,000 each.

This put him at risk for $6,500 including the vig (vigorish or tribute) on the 4 and 10. On the next roll of the dice, if the shooter made his point or any of the other five numbers, Arnold would collect his winnings, take down all his wagers, and walk away.

He went from casino to casino. He came home several thousand dollars ahead.

"Arnold," I said, "that's no system except for suicide! You can't overcome dice odds that way!"

Did you ever talk to a brick wall?

Arnold smiled benignly at me. What did I know?

All he knew was that he went back to Las Vegas and won again. And again.

You couldn't hold him down! Thousand-dollar bills were in circulation in those days and I remember that an aide accidentally spilled a tumbler of red wine on his bankroll which was piled high on his desk. He had to hang

63 thousand-dollar bills on his office radiator to dry out. It was quite a sight!

Then he made another journey to his easy-money land. This trip didn't begin well. He walked up to a table, waited until the shooter threw a point, then made his $6,500 worth of bets. The next roll was a seven.

He hurried to another table and did the same thing. The second roll was a 7. After it happened at the third table in the casino, he stumbled across the strip to another casino. It happened three times again. He came home a $39,000 loser.

Neither of us ever mentioned that "system" again.

THESE DAYS, Arnold Bruce Levy is a player who does well in Atlantic City because he has and follows a plan. He travels there by bus. He carries a 3 x 5 card to record what happens. It also acts to rein him in.

First he writes down on the card the name of the casino he is about to enter. Then, next to the name, he writes a modest number—usually $200 or $300. That's his immediate goal. He plays until he reaches the goal he set down for himself on the card and then he exits and hastens to the next casino.

I have known him to play in all twelve casinos in Atlantic City within ten hours. More often than not, he comes away a winner. Sometimes it's just a few hundred dollars. Sometimes it's as much as $4,000, $5,000 or more. And he does have his downs. No one can win every time.

Arnold never asks for credit from the casinos and he never writes checks. The result is that all he can lose is the money in his pocket, which he carefully limits.

This is one man whose years of experience have made him so goal-oriented that he is able to hit-and-run successfully.

Sometimes Arnold is in the city-by-the-sea no more than four hours, and then it's back to the Atlantic City bus terminal for the 2 1/2-hour ride back to Manhattan.

THERE WAS A particular cause to which I was eager to contribute. I decided to pick up some extra cash in Atlantic City.

I'd avoid the spotlight. No limo. No fancy suite. I drove to Atlantic City by myself. I walked to a blackjack table in the baccarat pit. I had a limit of $10,000. The pit boss picked up a phone and confirmed this.

I bet $9,000.

I was dealt a 16. The dealer showed a picture. That meant I had to draw. I drew a deuce. The dealer turned over a five. 15. He dealt himself a deuce. 17. My 18 beat him.

I cut my next wager to $6,000. If I lost, I would have been $4,000 ahead.

I was dealt an ace and a four. The dealer showed a five. I doubled down and received a 6. Total, 21.

The dealer turned over another 5. He drew a picture. Total, 20.

I picked up my $12,000 and asked for change of a black chip. I tipped the dealer $50.

I cashed in $10,000 and dropped the other chips into my jacket pockets. (If you cash more than $10,000 in any casino in Atlantic City during any 24-hour period, that casino is required to report you to the Treasury Department.)

WINNING ♦ AT ♥ CASINO ♠ GAMBLING ♣ 109

CASINO	SHOOT FOR	ACT	RT
TRUMP PLAZA	1000	(-2625)	(-2625)
CLARIDGE	1000	+1525	(-1100)

CASINO	SHOOT FOR	ACT.	RT
PARK PLACE	200	+175	+175
CLARIDGE	200	+450	+625
SANDS	200	+250	+875
RESORTS	200	+150	+1025
TAJ	200	+200	+1225
SHOWBOAT	200	+125	+1350
HARRAH	200	+325	+1675
T'S CASTLE	200	+325	+2000
GRAND	200	+175	+2175
TROP	200	+75	+2250
CAESAR	200	+75	+2325
T PLAZA	500	(-1425)	+900
CAESARS	200	+200	+1100
T PLAZA	1500	+900	+2000
CAESAR	200	(-400)	+1600
T PLAZA	500	+500	+2100

Here, for your amusement, are the cards reflecting Arnold's two recent forays. The top card reflects a 3-hour gaming session at only two casinos. Net loss: $1,100. The bottom card shows what happened two days later. Angry with himself at having set such a greedy goal of $1,000 a casino, he decided he'd play in all 12 of the gambling halls in Atlantic City but with goals limited to $200 per place. From 11:30 AM until 9:30 PM, Arnold Bruce Levy scurried from casino to casino, returning in the end to one or two where he'd already played. His net win was $2,100. Deduct the previous loss and Arnold was $1,000 ahead for the two visits.

Then I went to the hotel entrance and asked the valet for my car.

I drove home with a $21,970 profit, after tipping the valet $5. Deduct another $20 for gasoline. Deduct another $50 for turnpike tolls and automobile wear-and-tear.

I had a net profit of $21,900.

I had been in the casino for just about twenty minutes.

Anybody remember a philosophy called "hit and run?"

16

GOING WITH THE TREND

The information in the next few paragraphs can easily be worth at least one hundred times the cost of this book to anyone who risks more than ten dollars in a casino.

Irving Berlin wrote a song for a Fred Astaire film. The song, "Cheek to Cheek," refers to a gambler's lucky streak.

There *are* lucky streaks. These will be those times when you can do no wrong.

There are also unlucky streaks, during which time you won't be able to win a bet to save your butt.

I am indebted to Louis Holloway for the following rule. It has saved me several fortunes.

Let's use as an example a game I don't much play: roulette. The metal ball has fallen into a red number three times in a row. What do you do?

I'm certain half of my readers would chorus: "Bet black! Black is sure to come up!"

Wrong.

You have two choices. You bet on red, or you don't bet at all.

Why? Because one thing a sophisticated gambler knows is that *the improbable can happen.* Red could come up fifteen more consecutive times. Or fifty.

Three, for our purposes, is considered a streak.

You must bet with the streak or not at all.

If you bet with the streak and you're wrong, you'll lose one bet. If you bet against the streak and you're wrong, you can keep betting and betting and you can be wiped out.

This approach has a dual purpose. It allows you to get in on streaks, and it prevents you from becoming emotionally involved in bucking a trend.

If three passes are made at the crap tables, you bet with the shooter or not at all. If three shooters in a row miss (fail to make a pass), you bet on the "Don't pass" side or you don't bet at all.

At the baccarat table, if three hands in a row are Player (or Bank), you bet with that side or not at all.

I HAVE JUST saved you a lot of losing moments and cut down your chances of being sucked into a losing quicksand.

Gamblers have an advantage over non-gamblers. Quite apart from the thrills and the chills, one learns many life-lessons at the gaming tables. Gambling is fraught with uncertainty. Uncertainty is what life is all about.

One of those lessons is that in a casino, as in life, the improbable can happen and often does.

Let me illustrate.

I happen to be one of the world's worst poker players.

One night in a game of 7-card stud, a player who had joined the game for the first time had two queens showing.

I had a full house with kings, and the betting got hot and heavy. Ours was a table-stakes pot-limit game.

He turned up four queens.

The next hand, shuffled and dealt by a new dealer, using the alternate deck, gave me another neatly concealed full house—this time with aces! Again as the raising and re-raising heated up, the other players dropped out and I was facing the same opponent who had just beaten me for a lot of money with his four queens. I saw a delicious chance to recoup my loss as he bet into me.

I felt a delightful adrenaline rush. I raised back. Carefully. Enough to sucker him to re-raise. He did. Then I asked him to count his chips and I raised him for all the chips that sat in front of him, tapping him out. I tried to figure his hand but that didn't seem important. He showed three pictures which suggested either a straight or a flush. I had a lock. I was mentally totaling my win.

He called my bet.

"One thing I'm sure you don't have," I blithely remarked, "is four queens."

He had four queens.

The odds against a player having four queens twice in a row are astronomical. Literally millions to one. But that means that once in those millions of hands, someone somewhere will, indeed, have four queens twice in a row.

Respect the probability of the improbable.

THE SCENE WAS the baccarat table at the Aladdin. As the shoe went around the table, I built up my stake. Each time I had the shoe, I bet $4,000 on Bank. Four times the Player hand beat me with a natural nine.

The shoe was passed to me for the fifth time. I pushed forward my last $4,000 worth of chips.

"I don't care if I lose this one," I announced to one and all at the table, "but I'll be very annoyed if I lose it to another natural nine."

The other players smiled.

My hand was a natural eight. Worthless against the Player's eight and ace—another natural nine.

Five hands and each defeated by nine. $20,000 worth of experience in relearning that *the improbable is always possible.*

17

HOW TO GET RICH WITHOUT TRYING

I heard this story first-hand, but since I didn't actually see it happen, I offer it without sworn affidavits.

He's an elderly fellow in the meat-packing business and he's a fellow high-roller. And this is the story he told me.

"I'd had a losing session at a blackjack table, and I was on my way to the cashier cage to cash in my few remaining chips. Something was happening at a dice table that attracted my attention, because it was surrounded by a larger-than-usual crowd of spectators.

"A young man was shooting. Before he rolled, he kissed the dice; his girl kissed the dice and then he kissed his girl. It was an amusing ritual, and he went through it with every toss of the cubes.

"Suddenly I grasped the fact that he'd been doing it for a couple of minutes. The crowd loved every minute of it. I had $130 in my hand in chips. I placed the 6 and 8 for $60 each and pocketed the remaining two $5 chips.

"For a while, the young fellow threw almost nothing but 6s and 8s. I spread my profits to the other numbers.

"He threw the other numbers. By the time he sevened out, I needed five racks to hold my chips ($50,000) and I handed two blacks ($200) to the casino porter who helped pick up some of my chips that fell to the ground. The shooter had won a big $127, and I gave him $500."

The man who told me the story is not a braggart. He is a high-stakes player. As an experienced gambler, he had the instinct to get in on a hot roll.

Again and again you will observe that most players freeze as an improbably lucky streak takes place in front of their eyes. The experienced gambler has the instinct to jump in—even if it's in the middle. Even, in fact, if the next roll is the end of the streak. You may lose the bet, but you've done the correct thing.

THE STORY IS an old familiar one. It has happened from the first roll of the dice and the first turn of the playing cards.

Take this report from a subscriber to my own now-defunct newsletter *The High Roller.* The reader reported:

One night in February of this year at about 11 P.M., I wormed my way into a very crowded craps table in Caesars Palace with a stake of $500. The table was full of high rollers. Things got very cold and player after player left the table—but I was determined to stay until I threw the dice myself. By the time the cubes came to me I was the last player left at the table. I had $28 left of my $500. I then proceeded to make seventeen passes with a fair amount of numbers, and I won $15,000.

The same player continued:

During the roll, I made three elevens for the dealers at $25 a pop. This made me very popular with them and they were really rooting for me. I believe the roll could have been longer if my wife hadn't come over to ask, "How are you doing?" This to me was the kiss of death.

Let me relate an experience of mine. The place? The same casino. The time? Many years later.

It was New Year's Eve at Caesars Palace—or rather, about 5 A.M. New Year's Day. I walked from one dice table where I had just lost my self-determined limit for that table to another table where, as the shooter tossed the dice and they were still in the air, I shouted "$75 coming" and the dealer instinctively replied: "Bet."

But then he directed my attention to the little sign in front of him that said: Minimum bet, $100.

"There goes your three-unit system," the dealer said.

He knew my play: I always bet three units on the line so I can take maximum free odds behind the line.

I stood still. I hadn't been doing well and wasn't eager to bet blacks ($100 chips) instead of greens ($25 chips). But even while I was thinking about it, the young man to my right kept throwing number after number. I became aware that he was in the middle of a good shoot. I sprang into action. On and on he continued, tossing numbers and making points. It was a beautiful shoot and by the time he sevened out, I was a winner for the trip.

The dice were passed to me.

"I'm a hard act to follow," the young man said.

"You sure are," I said.

I placed three black chips on the line. Then I was off and running. Midway in my hand, someone at the other end of the table called "eleven" and flung a purple ($500) chip to the stickman. I threw an eleven.

"Same bet," he called, after being paid $7,500. I threw another eleven.

"Same bet," he called again. I threw a third eleven.

"Take me down," he said. He'd made profits of $21,000 on three rolls on what is regarded as a sucker bet because the odds are so heavily against it.

It was the improbable again.

When I sevened out, I left the table. At the cashier's cage a short gray-haired man and his wife approached me.

"I should kiss you," he said.

"Are you the guy with the elevens?" I asked.

"No. But I'm a guy who was a $12,000 loser even after that other fellow's hand, and you turned me into a winner!"

HIS NAME IS Sheldon Kneller and he's the surgeon who saved my wife Carole's life when she was thrown from a horse and punctured a lung and broke several ribs.

We'd become friends and we were sharing a room at the Pritikin Longevity Center in Santa Monica. Weekends are quiet there and Sheldon had never been to Las Vegas so I invited him to fly there as my guest.

We took the short flight early Saturday morning. We taxied from the airport directly to the Horseshoe on

Fremont Street. I'm much attracted by their "10 times odds" in craps.

The casino was uncommonly quiet but it was early. I stepped up to a craps table that had only two other players. A man at the other end of the table was tossing the dice. I dropped a few $100 bills on the green felt and said, "Change only."

I was impatient. I would be the next shooter and I was eager to throw the dice.

Suddenly it occurred to me that the guy at the opposite end was having a decent shoot. I quickly placed a few numbers and made the first of a series of come bets that would allow me to take ten times odds.

By the time the shooter sevened out, I had pulled in profits of more than $9,000.

"Is it your turn now?" Sheldon asked as the stickman pushed five dice toward me so I could select two.

"Hell no!" I said. "I've just done all the gambling I'm going to do today! I've won our air fare. I've won the cost of Pritikin. That's it! Now I'll show you some of the interesting sights in town."

Did I get in on the streak instead of standing there like a dummy? Yes. Did I keep my word about not doing any more gaming that day? Yes.

THE MORAL TO the above anecdotes? When you think somebody is lucky-streaking, don't just stand there. *Do something!*

18

PLAIN TALK ABOUT DICE

The exercise I'm about to describe should be a "must" for everyone who gambles serious money at a craps table.

First, get yourself a pair of casino dice. You can buy a pair at most casino-city newsstand shops and novelty shops for $1—or, ask your favorite casino. Many will give you a souvenir pair for the asking.

At home, to prepare yourself, get a clean white sheet of paper and a pen or pencil.

Next, toss the dice against your pillow or on the floor against the wall. Make sure at least one die hits the pillow or the wall each time. Write down the numbers after each toss.

Throw the dice 144 times. That's 36 x 4. Then examine the results.

You may be startled. And you may begin to have some real understanding of what dice are all about.

THERE ARE 36 possible combinations with two dice. If they all turn up, the following will be close to the results of your 144 dice throws:

2: (1 and 1) will turn up four times.

3: (2 and 1, 1 and 2) will turn up eight times.

4: (3 and 1, 1 and 3, 2 and 2) will turn up twelve times.

5: (3 and 2, 2 and 3, 4 and 1, 1 and 4) will turn up sixteen times.

6: (3 and 3, 4 and 2, 2 and 4, 5 and 1, 1 and 5) will turn up twenty times.

7: (6 and 1, 1 and 6, 5 and 2, 2 and 5, 4 and 3, 3 and 4) will turn up twenty-four times.

8: (4 and 4, 6 and 2, 2 and 6, 5 and 3, 3 and 5) will turn up twenty times.

9: (6 and 3, 3 and 6, 5 and 4, 4 and 5) will turn up sixteen times.

10: (5 and 5, 6 and 4, 4 and 6) will turn up twelve times.

11: (6 and 5, 5 and 6) will turn up eight times.

12: (6 and 6) will turn up four times.

WHAT I'VE JUST described is elementary knowledge for experienced craps players, so, dear reader, please be patient with this sole gesture to the uninitiated.

Those possible combinations are what make for dice odds. In thirty-six rolls, the probability is that:

7 will come up 6 times, to the 5 times that a 6 or 8 will come up, so the true odds are 6 to 5.

7 will come up 6 times, to the four times that a 5 or 9 will come up, so the true odds are 6 to 4 or 3 to 2.

7 will come up 6 times, to the three times that a 4 or 10 will come up, so the true odds are 2 to 1.

Over any extended period of play the house will grind the player out because the casino has an advantage of 1.41 percent on the "Do" side and slightly less on the "Don't" side.

YOUR 144 THROWS of the dice should be remarkable in their resemblance to the proper odds.

What should this teach you?

Namely, that the numbers do tend to come up close to their mathematical probabilities. Only their sequence varies, and herein lies your hope.

Analyze your 144 throws as if you had been wagering on the shooter.

Now analyze them as if you were a "Don't" bettor. Then analyze them following the "three-is-a-trend" philosophy so that if three shooters didn't make a pass, you switched to "Don't pass."

If you aren't willing to do this little exercise, then you should stay away from the dice tables.

I did the exercise for you in my first book. I've done it again for this one. But looking at my scoreboard isn't going to teach you as effectively as doing it yourself.

On the opposite page is the sequence in which my dice tosses came up when I threw them against a pillow on my bed in Stuyvesant, New York on September 3rd of this year, assisted by my wife, Carole, who recorded the results:

144 ROLLS OF THE DICE

7*
8 11 7*
11*
4 6 9 8 10 10 6 7*
5 9 7*
9 11 10 12 8 5 9*
11*
6 9 7 10 3 7*
8 8*
12*
4 3 6 8 6 7*
4 4 2 4*
6 8 4 11 7*
4 6 7*
4 7 10 9 6 3 5 6 5 5 4*
6 8 9 11 7*
7*
5 8 11 5*
5 11 5*
10 3 9 11 11 2 10*
10 4 10*
5 10 5*
7*
5 11 11 7 10 2 3 8 4 8 9 2 8 7*
4 10 9 5 8 6 9 5 8 7*
5 8 8 10 6 8 4 9 11 7*
7*
9 11 11 10 7*
8 3 7 10 3 7*
8 9 11 8*
8 7*
11*
7*
6 6*

---

* indicates a decision

WHAT CAN YOU learn from these results?

Well, for one thing, there were 34 decisions. That means a decision every 4.2 tosses of the dice. Wagering on the pass line, you would have won 19 hands and lost 15. However, if you'd been betting on the "Don't" side you'd have won only 14 of the hands in view of the "Bar 12" rule.

I compared this with a similar chart that I prepared 17 years ago. At that time, there was a decision for every 3 3/7 tosses of the dice. In that showing, if you bet on the pass line, you would have won 20 hands and lost 23. The Don't-pass bettor would have won only 20 of his wagers because "12" was the "come out" number three times. In 1978 an extra roll was necessary to complete the last hand.

Now, here is how the numbers came up against probabilities:

NUMBER	SHOULD HAVE COME UP	CAME UP 1978	CAME UP 1994
2	4	3	4
3	8	8	7
4	12	13	11
5	16	17	15
6	20	22	15
7	24	23	24
8	20	16	20
9	16	16	14
10	12	9	15
11	8	12	17
12	4	5	2
	144	144	144

Notice that sevens came up according to probability: exactly once for every six rolls. This shoot was 11-rich and thus some other numbers were short of their probability appearances.

A final observation: probability is a prediction, based on mathematics, of what *may* happen. It doesn't mean it *must* happen or that it always will happen.

Don't settle for what you've just read.

Do it yourself!

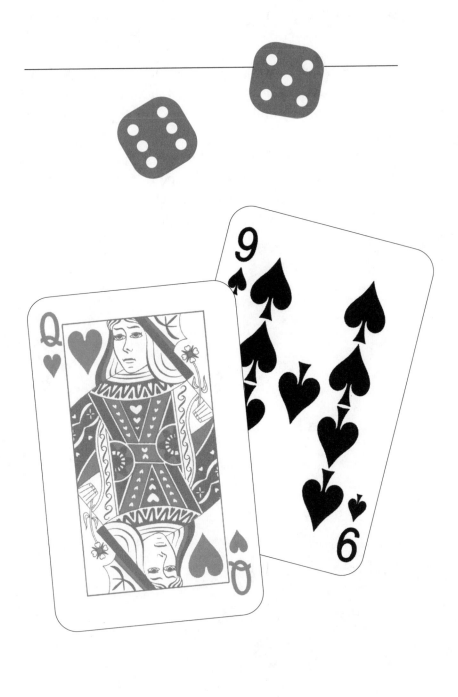

19

ROLL THEM BONES!

Craps may well be the oldest known gambling game in human history. Roman soldiers tossed the cubes. So did the Egyptians. The game probably originated with the cave man.

Craps (once called "Kraps") and roulette are the two most random games in the casino. Think about it: the scenarios for blackjack and baccarat are altered with each card dealt. In craps, every roll is a truly independent event. Dice have no eyes and no memory of past rolls. They have no feelings. They don't know or care who throws them.

In harmony with my "hit-and-run" philosophy, I believe you can spend only a limited time at the dice tables if you want to walk away a winner. For that reason I believe in larger wagers for quick decisions. The more you linger, the more you lose.

An acknowledged mathematical genius named Jess Marcum (known as the "little dark-haired guy" in Ed Thorp's classic book, *Beat the Dealer*), examined time as a key factor in winning and losing. He found that if you started with $1,000 and were to wager $1 on every hand for two months without stopping, you'd have one chance in two *trillion* to win $1,000 before you lost your $1,000.

On the other hand if you limited your playing time to less than one half-hour and if you bet $200 each time, you'd increase your odds for winning $1,000 from 2-trillion-to-one, to 1.15-to-one.

What conclusion does this bring you to? My "hit-and-run" philosophy again! Want to win $1,000? Send it sailing in as a single bet. You win it or you lose it. The fat lady has sung! End of drama!

The casino would much prefer that you make hundreds of smaller bets so they can grind you out.

THERE'S ONE HAND in dice when you have odds against the casino, but for that roll only.

That's the "come-out" roll, of course.

On that first roll, the "Pass line " or "Come" bettor has a 2-1 edge over the casino because there are six ways seven can come up (6-1, 1-6, 5-2, 2-5, 4-3, 3-4) and two ways 11 can come up (6-5, 5-6) giving you eight chances to double your money on the first roll.

Against you are the 2 "snake eyes," 1-1) the 3 craps (2-1, 1-2) and the 12 ("Box cars," 6-6) and these add up to four hands that will take away your money.

To reemphasize the value of free odds, I'll point out here that a bet on the pass line with ten-times odds cuts the casino's advantage to 0.18 percent, as against a bet with no free odds which has 1.41 percent going against you. When you buck the 1.41 percent, each $5 bet costs you 7-1/2 cents.

CRAPS IS NO longer the prime table game in casinos. Although you may still see lots of crowded crap tables, the number of crapshooters declines as the years hurry by.

World War II was the era in which men and women in the armed forces learned to shoot dice. Before that, we learned the rules in pool halls or in alleyways.

That generation—my generation—still accounts for most of the action at crap tables. There is no new schoolroom for craps and few young people are learning the game.

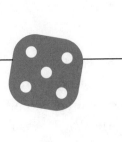

20

LET'S TALK MONEY
MANAGEMENT

Before you saunter up to the dice table—or the baccarat table—or seat yourself on a comfortable stool at a blackjack table,—be sure you've assimilated Rule Five.

This one is so simple and obvious that if you have ever done any real gambling it will seem like a kindergarten lesson:

PUT LIMITS ON POSSIBLE LOSSES
FOR EACH SESSION
—AND STICK TO THEM

Let us imagine that your total stake is $2,000. Before you walk to the table, fix firmly in your own mind your maximum initial loss for the foray. Let's say you decide to risk $200. You may, if you wish, mentally fix another $100 as a reserve.

If chance isn't kissing you; if lady luck isn't blowing happiness up your trouser leg or your skirt—and you lose the $200 but have the feeling (the feeling, not the hope) that things will change, and you feel you are more in tune with what's happening, risk the other $100.

If that goes, *walk.*

If you can't obey this simple task of self-discipline, then the following may be true:

1. You can't control yourself—and someone out-of-control has no place in a casino playing with real money. Stay home and play video games on your television screen instead.

2. You don't *really* want to win.

THE BOOK you're holding is not intended to be a psychology primer or a self-help guide to knowing yourself. But that second question is the key to everything.

Do you really want to win?

Silly question?

Not at all. You would be amazed at the things that motivate people in their gambling. And you would be amazed at how many feel clean and purified after losing but feel terribly uncomfortable when they are winning.

Clean? Yes, *clean!* You've heard the expression, "I took a bath."

Think about it. DO YOU REALLY WANT TO WIN?

Keep reminding yourself that *the contest is between you and yourself and not you and the casino.*

And keep reminding yourself that you're there not to play but *to win.*

Ask yourself if you *really* want to win and then sit quietly and let your true feelings surface. What *are* those feelings? Is the answer "yes" or "I don't know" or "not really" or "no"?

If the answer is YES and you genuinely want to leave casino-land with more money than you had when you arrived, you have to pay some dues.

You've got to constantly remind yourself that

YOU ARE NOT IN THE CASINO
TO ENJOY YOURSELF.

The pleasure of profits should be enjoyment enough for you. Let others have the fun at the games.

And they do. Casino customers are flattered by the expensive surroundings. Most of them lose money on every trip to a gaming-land. They lose and yet they're pleased by the experience of being treated with respect by dealers.

Whether it's a Mississippi riverboat or an Indian reservation-turned-gold-mine, the customers find relief from boredom. There are some who believe it's a satisfactory substitute for success. (Not for me, it isn't!)

YOU AREN'T there to play games, see shows, eat good food or lounge in royal suites. All that is for the gullible guppies who fill the casinos like schools of fish waiting to be hooked and reeled in. All casino strategy is designed to chloroform the human lollipops so they can be separated from their money as painlessly as possible.

Reread the above paragraph. It is so critical—so valuable— that I would have printed it in gold leaf, if I could have.

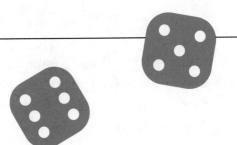

21

A POSITIVE APPROACH

TO CRAPS

L et's get into your actual dice play.

By now you've tossed the dice 144 times at home, made a record of the results and studied them. You also are totally acquainted with the true odds.

Before you bet Dollar One, be sure you know and understand the house rules. Don't be shy. As my Japanese friend Misa Ban says, "Is money concerned." She doesn't mean it as a question. It's a statement on the realities of life and should alert you to key in on your own self-interest.

Don't be shy about asking questions. Remember, "Is money concerned."

What is the casino's maximum bet? Its minimum? Does the house allow double odds? Triple odds? Five times odds? Ten?

LET'S TALK ABOUT ODDS and take a moment to examine how place bets are paid off. I meet veteran crap shooters who, even today, don't understand it.

When you place a number, the first unit you place will be paid off at even money. The other units will be paid at true odds. For example, you place five chips on "5." A "5" is thrown. You get one chip (even money) for your bottom chip and the other four are paid off at 3-to-2, true odds against a 5. Thus you've won seven chips.

I SAID EARLIER that my play is to place three units* on the line. If I can get five or ten times odds, I bet one unit. When a number becomes a point, I take the maximum free odds.

I play with three units because that allows me maximum free odds. The free (true) odds bet is the only no-odds-against-you wager the casino offers you.

Take my word on this one: at the infinite dice game, the casino makes no money on odds be they single, double, triple or ten times.

In theory, over an extended period of time neither you nor the casino will benefit by the wager. It's pure break-even. In reality, this is one place where, when you are running right, you can make the most profit for each dollar at risk.

Let's say you're playing with green chips ($25).

With three chips ($75) on the line: if you throw a 4 or 10 you put another three chips ($75) behind the line. These pay 2-to-1.

With three chips ($75) on the line: if you throw a 5 or 9 you place 4 chips ($100) behind the line. These pay 3-to-2.

With 3 units ($75) on the line: if you throw a 6 or 8 you put five units ($125) behind the line. These pay 6-to-5.

---

*$1, $5, $25, $100, $500—the level of your play doesn't matter. It's 3 of whatever unit chips you're betting.

In every case you can be sure you can quickly make certain you're being paid correctly because the payoff is always 9 units. (With $25 chips that would be $225.)

Simple, yes?

What then are double odds?

Some years ago a young fellow named Bill Friedman saw that he couldn't beat blackjack in a way that would allow him to live in style, so he decided to become a management expert. He taught well-attended courses at the University of Nevada on how to run a casino.

Then he wrote a book for me titled *Casino Management.* The most recent edition was priced at $125 a copy. Bill told me the book's publication opened the door to a general manager's job with the Summa Corporation, owned by Howard Hughes. Bill was assigned to manage its "stiff," a small hotel-casino named the Castaways. Small? For a long time the casino had only one dice table.

No fancy showroom. No gourmet dining room. Not even a lounge show. How then to attract players?

Are you ready?

Bill Friedman built a parking lot. A *parking lot!* The advantage was that you could park your own car and walk directly from the lot into the casino. No waiting. No valet tips. No long walks. No lobbies to lumber through.

But Bill did more than that. He announced the highest payoff in town on dollar slot machines and free *double odds* on dice.

Others watched closely as Friedman turned the Castaways into the most profitable-per-dollar-invested-casino in the Hughes collection of seven. Then he also managed the Silver Slipper. That's two.

When the casinos were sold to be torn down, one became part of the site of The Mirage and the other is now being built into a freeway next to the Frontier.

Bill became a highly paid consultant. In two instances, he turned down a $250,000 "on signing" bonus offered by wealthy businessmen who bought casinos. Bill told the men in both instances that their casinos were doomed and nothing could save them.

As usual, he was right.

WHAT ARE FREE double odds?

Let me explain why my line bets are 3 units. In an ordinary game, I bet 3 units on the line. You know now (but it's worth repeating) that if you throw a 4 or 10, you back it up with 3 units; a 5 or 9 with 4 units, and a 6 or 8 with 5 units.

With double odds you can back a 4, 5, 9 or 10 with 6 units and (in most double odds casinos) a 6 or 8 with 7-1/2 units.

This is what it means in payoffs:

4 or 10. You bet 3 on the line and 6 behind. If the shooter throws the number before throwing a 7, you are paid a total of 24 units for a profit of 15. You get back the 3 you bet on the line, plus even money for that part of the winning wager. You get back the 6 you bet behind the line, plus the true 2-to-1 odds of another 12 units.

And so forth for the other numbers.

At first I was skeptical. The access to free double odds meant that the house was cutting its percentage from 1.41 to .6. Why should they do that?

Some believe it's to induce you to bet more money and thus knock you out of the box more rapidly. This is based on the belief that the less time a player stands at a table, the less chance he has to catch a streak. (I don't happen to buy this one.)

I approached Bill Friedman and asked him for his casino philosophy.

"Purely competitive," he said. "If every casino did it, we'd lose our edge."

What it means, of course, is that if you bet a series of winning bets you'll win much more money much more quickly. But if you lose, you'll lose more money more rapidly, too.

Your choice.

Want to know mine? These days I won't play any place where I'm offered only single odds.

Here is one part of my play that is rigid: I never make a bet unless I have the dollars and the determination to back it with fullest allowable free odds. If you don't do this, you are giving the house an unnecessary edge against you and you might as well quit now.

Repeat: Never make a line bet or a come bet that you are not willing and able to back up with the full available free odds.

If you lose your nerve because the results are going against you, walk away from the table. Give yourself a chance to build your resolve by focusing on something else for a while. Play nickel slot machines. See a lounge show. Watch TV. Read a newspaper or magazine. Read a book.

Why should you care about maximum bet limits? I'll give you the reason right here.

Sometime, when things are not going well with you and you seem to be getting ground out, you might want to make one large wager to see if in a single win you can recover your losses.

It's a bold move, but no more dangerous than standing still while you are being ground down.

Also, sometime you might get lucky and, while lucky, you may want to press your luck. You should know in advance where the ceiling is.

At the moment, some casinos in Atlantic City offer five-times odds. In Las Vegas, several casinos, including the Frontier and Bob Stupak's Vegas World, copy Binion's Horseshoe by offering ten-times free odds. I feel a slight sense of futility telling you these specifics since they can change even before you read this page.

IN JUNE OF this year, my wife and I had an hour to kill before checking in at the Las Vegas airport. We didn't have time to drive downtown but we could drive a couple of casinos away to the Frontier. The marquee of the Frontier announced "10 x odds."

Somehow we couldn't find the entrance and found ourselves in the rear where we had to wake up a valet who asked incredulously, "You want to *park*?"

It was a long walk from the back of the hotel to the casino. As we walked through, I saw that the limit at black-jack was $1,000. I pulled a small clump of $100 bills out of my pocket, placed them in a betting spot and said, "Money plays." I didn't count the money.

I won the hand. The dealer counted out $700. Nice beginning.

I picked up my cash and the chips I'd won, and we headed for the craps pit. There were five tables and all five were bursting with action.

Big action?

I'd never seen this before in a Strip casino. Most of the players were betting $1 on the line and $10 behind the line. Only one other fellow and myself were using greens ($25) and blacks ($100).

I looked at my watch. Carole said she didn't want to shoot. "Okay, I'll shoot when the dice come around to me, and then we'll head for the airport."

My stake went up and down with no meaningful dips or surges.

The dice passed to a woman on my right. I would be next.

The lady tossed the dice. She threw. And she threw. And she threw.

I began playing small ($10 and $100 odds) but soon realized that the lady on my right was having a real shoot. I upped my bets to $20 and $200 odds. Eventually I was betting $30 and taking $300 odds.

And she continued to throw.

I turned to Carole. "We don't have time for me to shoot. Let's just wait until she sevens out and we'll get out of here."

But she didn't seven out. The only sevens she threw were on her come out rolls.

And she threw and threw and threw.

Getting anxious about the time, I pulled down $900 worth of place bets. "I'll cash in," I told Carole. "You get the car so we'll have a head start." I handed her the parking ticket and hurried to the cashier cage.

The reaction? One would think I'd broken the bank at Monte Carlo. I had $4,200 in chips. They were counted. Then on the phone they were described by denomination.

The cashier waited for a confirming call. Then she counted out the cash. I reached for it but she stayed my hand, saying "I have to count it twice!"

I suppose the casino has to win a lot of $1 bets to equal a $4,200 loss.

The transaction took more than ten minutes. With the cash in my pocket, I started to run through the casino to the rear entrance. I glanced at the tables. The lady was still throwing the dice!

We returned to New York at midnight. In bed, at 1:30 A.M. I tapped Carole on the shoulder: "I just got the feeling that she just sevened out!"

22

THE CASINO REVOLUTION

L as Vegas has changed from the time it was a lonely railroad water-stop boasting a few saloons that featured gambling. When Bugsy Siegel built the Flamingo it was the third casino on the Strip. The Flamingo had 105 rooms. (Today, Hilton-owned, it has 3,642. Even the unflappable Bugsy would have been impressed with what he started.) Casinos sprouted up from the desert sands and Las Vegas became Casino City. But the nation still looked critically at gamblers.

In part, the rapid change in social prohibitions against gaming, began, as I suggested, with the legalization of State lotteries. No longer true was the witticism of Ambrose Bierce that "The gambling known as business looks with austere disdain at the business known as gambling."

Newspaper publisher Hank Greenspun started the historic turning point when he persuaded Howard Hughes to move to Las Vegas. There, the eccentric billionaire hermit settled in a suite on the penthouse floor of the Desert Inn. He rented the balance of the floor for his Mormon aides.

When the Desert Inn's owners asked him to leave so gamblers could occupy the costly suites, Hughes said, "Buy it."

"Buy what?" an aide asked.

"The hotel and the casino."

"How much should we pay for it, Mr. Hughes?" the aide asked.

"Whatever it takes," he was told.

So it was bought.

HUGHES' CONTRIBUTION to the casino revolution is that he gave gambling the imprimatur of respectability. He made bold promises to the people of Nevada, few of which he kept. But he was a prominent American industrialist, and he was investing in gambling casinos.

Now Las Vegas was beginning to have a corporate face.

Caesars Palace opened its doors and became the "in" spot, luring the big players to its portals. The Palace is owned by Caesars World. That corporation enjoyed its first billion-dollar year in 1993, although its profits dropped from $83,215,000 to $78,361,000. (Slot action, where there are few variables, had the highest action and made more money for the casino than it had ever made before.)

How could there be a drop in profits? Costs rise but not that much. The fact is that the casino was "damaged" several times by "whales" who knew when to talk and when to walk and walked away with several million dollars in winnings.

A "whale" is the label given to high rollers who can drop a million dollars or more on a single visit. Just one of them can make a casino's weekend "good" or "bad." Many a night has seen a chunk of Caesars World earnings walk out the door when a big gambler hits a streak at baccarat at Caesars Palace.

By contrast, those people who "buy in" for ten or twenty dollars and then talk their heads off to pit bosses hoping to scrounge RFBs (room, food and beverage comps) are called "fleas" by dealers and pit bosses.

Keep in mind that a high roller can lose more money in twenty minutes than four busloads of housewives and retired plumbers tugging at slot machine handles can lose in an entire afternoon. And once in a while, not every day but once in a while, the whales go away winners.

THE CASINO revolution came with the arrival of Steve Wynn. He and William Bennett, the 70-year-old force who was recently toppled from his role as Circus Circus Enterprises by disgruntled stockholders. Wynn and Bennett are the two men with the daring and vision to build (or rebuild) cash-flow cows such as Golden Nugget, Circus Circus, The Mirage, The Luxor,* Treasure Island and The Excalibur.

Kirk Kerkorian outdid everyone with the MGM Grand. Under the direction of Larry Woolf, it is a self-contained palace of pleasure.

Now Las Vegas was not merely hotels with adjoining casinos.

---

*The Luxor, owned by Circus Circus, seems a depressing place to me. It so depends on low-rollers that for months after it opened it had neither a credit department nor a credit manager. There was a $1,000 limit at its blackjack tables. The whole place seems to me to be a spoof of the new trend in elaborate casinos.

Wynn's Mirage Resorts has four major properties in Las Vegas and several joint ventures outside of the U.S. The 29-story Mirage sits on 100 acres and its offspring, Treasure Island, sits on another 17 acres. The two share some of their property for parking.

While the dream palaces were going up in Vegas, things were happening in other parts of the nation, too. Like Atlantic City. Like the Indian Gaming Regulatory Act (IGRA) of 1988. Like the Mississippi riverboats, the fastest-growing segment of gaming in 1974. (The Gulf Coast has ten casinos within 25 miles of each other.)

In 1993 more than 900,000 visitors flew directly to Atlantic City. Its International Airport features 28 flights each day by scheduled airlines. In addition, it offers many commuter and charter flights.

FRONT-RUNNERS like Wynn and Bennett found they had to look over their shoulders. More than 60 Indian tribes made arrangements to open casinos. The announced purpose was "to make it easier for economically depressed native Americans to improve their lot."

They are certainly doing that! Their casinos are more than wigwams. According to a report in *The New York Times*, Indian gaming grossed $15.2 billion in 1993.

The 1988 Federal Indian Gaming Regulatory Act seems to give every tribe the right to open a casino on its reservation. At which point you're not looking at the level playing field of Eton. As I pointed out earlier, the reservations don't have to open their books to the public, don't pay Federal taxes, and are much less regulated than non-Indian casinos.

Steve Wynn is currently the hero of Las Vegas. Whether he'll continue to be so after the revelations in the forthcoming book, *Running Scared*, remains to be seen. This unauthorized biography, now being written by 4th-generation Nevadan John Smith, is scheduled to be published in the spring of 1995.

You don't fool with Steve Wynn. His power and influence extend far beyond the portals of his gambling palaces. Last year Ray Cuddy masterminded the kidnapping of Wynn's daughter. Cuddy was caught, Ms. Wynn was found unharmed, and rueful Ray was sentenced to 24 1/2 years in prison.

Steve Wynn isn't suffering. He can always go to his Shadow Creek golf course. You can't. You can't pay a greens fee or bribe the starter. Only Steve Wynn's close friends or those who have million-dollar lines of credit are allowed to step onto the pristine green. The course, built quietly at a reported cost of $30 million, is, in effect, Wynn's private playground.

Why so much money to build a golf course? Blame it on the cost of acreage. My old friend Nick Darvas (he wrote *Wall Street, The Other Las Vegas*) once bought some Las Vegas land on the cheap. Each dollar of his investment became $1,000. A $600 land parcel brought him an offer of $600,000.

Some of the land he didn't buy included part of the 164-acre parcel that Steve Wynn recently acquired for $400,000 an acre. Kirk Kerkorian paid $2 million an acre for the land parcel that fronts on the Strip and Tropicana.

ATLANTIC CITY HAS become loud-mouthed, publicity-hungry Donald Trump's stomping ground. He heads three casinos including the gigantic Taj Mahal.

To know The Donald is not to like him.

His inflated ego makes him imagine that he competes with Wynn and Bennett. It's all in his imagination. A reality check will tell you that his vanity and ignorance are only exceeded by his lack of talent. The Taj Mahal reflects this in its coldness and lack of humor.

The only thing to his credit is that he's not pulling down a management fee similar to that of some of his rivals. For example, Arthur M. Goldberg, an attorney, backed into the casino industry when he took a large position in Bally Entertainment stock and then, after a fight, seized control of the chain to protect his investment. Goldberg's total compensation for 1993 was $9,468,059. This included such things as "incentives" and stock options.

Caesars World boss-man Henry Gluck was the 5th largest earner with $4,170,422.

Contrast this with Steve Wynn whose Mirage Resorts paid him a mere $2,513,389.

Well, they didn't really pay it to him. You did, with your losses at his tables and slots.

LAS VEGAS HAS SOLD America the image that it's a family destination. Sure, there are children aplenty among the twenty-four million annual visitors. But "family" most often means that players bring their brothers, sisters, Aunt Helen and Mom and Dad.

23

DICING UP CASINO-LAND

In 1990 the American Booksellers Association scheduled its once-a-year convention in Las Vegas. I was asked to write an article for *Publishers Weekly*, the book industry's trade magazine.

My article was called *Fun and Gaming in Las Vegas*. In it, I pointed out that casinos on Fremont Street offered the best deals. I wrote "These are called 'sawdust joints'. Sinatra doesn't sing here and beluga caviar may be difficult to locate, but these side-by-side casinos offer better odds, lots of freebies and a more relaxed atmosphere than on the Strip."

A recent report on the slot win, for example, showed that the downtown casinos paid out 95.3 percent as against the Strip casinos' 94.6 percent

Nineteen casinos in downtown Las Vegas had gaming revenue in excess of a million dollars. On the Strip, the 32 largest casinos showed profits of $593,755,945. This averages out to $18,554,873 per casino.

A WORD ABOUT Binion's Horseshoe, my favorite down-town place. It's the only casino I know where the owners are true gamblers. Benny Binion couldn't read or write, but he had smarts beyond his education, and he was tough. They tell a story of his appearance before his parole board when he was in prison. The chairman reviewed his record. "You killed a man named so-and-so?"

"Yeah," admitted Benny. "He was making noise at the bar and I tussled with him and my pistol went off."

There was a similar response when the parole board cited another killing. Then they a referred to a third.

"Aw, you're not gonna hold that one against me too!" he protested. "That guy wasn't even white!"

Was tough old Benny Binion a racist? Not really. His closest friend was an African-American.

BENNY BINION'S son Jack now runs The Horseshoe. Jack will allow maximum bets equal to the customer's first wager. By prior arrangement, that first wager can be as much as $1,000,000. (John "Bet-a-million" Gates would have loved it!)

Ten years ago Jack Binion received a phone call. A drawling voice at the other end wanted to know if the offer was true "or just publicity."

Jack assured him it was true.

A few hours later, a shabbily dressed man arrived with a large grocery shopping bag and dumped $770,000 on a craps table. After the dealers counted the money and ver-ified the total, the man turned to Jack Binion: "That's my first wager. I wanna bet it all on the Don't side."

Jack gave him a single special chip.

"You're faded," Jack said.

The man picked up the dice. He tossed a six. Then an eight. Then a nine. Then he sevened out.

Binion paid off the cowboy's bet with $1,540,000.

They didn't even ask his name.*

One of the awed spectators asked him: "How could you bet so much on one hand?"

"Aw," the man explained, "inflation was eatin' away at my money so I decided to either double it or lose it all."

Ten months later the man returned. He identified himself as William Lee Bergstrom. This time he bet one million dollars on a single craps hand.

He lost.

Victor Lownes would say, "I told you so."

When Victor ran the Playboy casino in London, his philosophy was that when someone leaves the casino as a big winner, he is just making a loan from the casino. In time he'll return and repay the loan with high interest.

Another man from London, Chris Boyd, a casino programmer, is trying to challenge Victor's thesis. He saved for three years and early this year he managed to put together $230,000. He arrived at the Horseshoe, dressed in a tuxedo.

He asked that the "00" be blocked out and Jack Binion agreed. Then he received permission to bet it all on one roll

---

*That was before the IRS inflicted those rules on casinos about reporting winners. They are more rigid in Atlantic City, where, as I mentioned earlier, if you cash $1 more than $10,000 in a casino in any 24-hour period, the casino must report you to the United States Treasury. In Las Vegas, there are less rigid rules and Nevada is not required to report verifiable winnings.

of the roulette wheel. (Caesars Palace had turned him down when he offered to make the same wager with them.)

Boyd asked for and was granted a practice run. But after only one spin, when the ball landed on zero, he placed his $230,000 chip on red. He waited nervously as the ball spun around, seeming to take an interminable time to land in 7. Red.

Incidentally, the Horseshoe usually limited even-money wagers on the roulette wheel to $100,000. But they made this exception when Boyd told them how he'd tried every casino in London and not one of them would book his bet.

I ENJOY TAKING ten times odds at The Horseshoe even as my friend, Arnold Boston, argues that the free odds don't reduce the odds against the player. He insists that the lower percentages are, in fact, an illusion.

It depends on how you look at it. In theory, free odds is an even-money bet against the house. As I explained, in theory, in the long run, neither side has an advantage.

But let's examine it in simple practical dollar terms. Let's say you have $30 to bet. You bet it on the line and throw a 4 (or 10). No free odds. You will make the 4 (or 10) once in three hands and lose it twice.

Wager: $90. Return: $60.

Instead you bet $15 on the line, throw 4 (or 10) and take $15 odds. Again, you will win only once in three hands. But you receive two-to-one for your odds money.

Wager: $90. Return: $75.

Now, instead, you take double free odds.

You bet $10 on the line, throw a 4 (or 10) and take $20 double odds. You will win, on average, the same one in three hands.

Wager: $90. Return: $80.

Or take my favorite: 10 times free odds. You bet $3 on the line and take $27 free odds. You will win, on average, the same once in three hands.

Wager $90. Return $87.

You're wagering the same amount of money in all cases but, for example, on the particular point of 4 (or 10) you come away with $60 on a line no-odds bet, $80 on a line with double odds bet, and $87 on a 10-times-free odds encounter.

Of course you won't take down as much money on a come out roll of 7 or 11, or lose as much on a 2, 3, or 12.

THERE IS A CONSTANT rope-tug between reality and superstition.

Most dice players will repeat some of the things I spoke of earlier: belief that when dice hit a hand or a die jumps off the table, there is a likelihood that the next roll will be 7-out.

I, too, believed things like that. For years.

One day I decided to find out, for sure. I was curious about whether the belief came about because one is vividly aware of hunches that come true but quickly forgets them when they don't. I began to keep records.

Sevens should come up an average of once in six rolls. I observed that hitting a hand or bouncing onto the floor had no statistical effect on the number of times 7 came up on the next roll. You can forget that. If, on the other hand, you feel comfortable taking off your odds and everything else that will come off after a die goes off the table, etc., by all means do it. Always do that which you are most comfortable doing.

OBSERVE THE loser in action.

He'll make a line bet. That's the good one. He doesn't follow the 3-unit rule because he doesn't take full odds and maybe doesn't even understand them.

Now he'll throw money to the stickman for "c & e" (craps and eleven) or "any craps." As soon as a point is thrown, he'll cover the hard ways.

He's a dice desperado and his good 1.41 percent bet on the line has been drowned in a flood of foolishness. His dollars* are headed for the waterfall that will carry them into the casino counting room.

Once in a while Joe or Juliet Sucker will feel glamorous hitting a long shot on the center layout play. But the wins are soon swallowed by the law of averages, and the player will go away blaming a run of "bad luck."

Casino managers love you to make proposition bets. Stickmen are trained to promote them. There is nothing puzzling about this. Proposition bets give the house a larger advantage against you than do line bets.

Proposition bets are wretched bets. Let's take the example of the wager on "any craps" that pays 7-to-1. Let's

---

*Very often I talk in terms of dollars rather than chips. Changing chips for your dollars is the narcotic they give you—the first step on the way to emptying your pockets.

say that I have $300 on the line. I bet an additional $50 on "any craps." The dice come out and total 2, 3 or 12.

Craps! I lose my $300 line bet. The stickman instructs the dealer to give me $350. My original $50 bet is now working on the next roll. (If I take it down, I have a flat $50 profit.)

Sounds good, right?

Except that "any craps" will come up only once in eight times. If you make the bet consistently and the numbers come up in proper probability over any period of time, you will wager $1,800 and receive in return a total of $1,600.

This means you will lose an average of $200 if you make the wager 36 times.

Odds against you: 11.11 percent.

Is it any wonder that the dealer keeps intoning, "Make a bet on craps?"

Are proposition bets ever worthwhile? Sure.

Gambling legend Mannie Kimmel used to beat the proposition layout in an interesting way. He carried a small counting machine in each trouser pocket. He'd stand at the table as an observer, hands in his pockets. He would clock a long series of dice rolls until one number didn't show up for a while. He favored 2s, 11s, and 12s.

When one of those hadn't appeared in a long time (as for example, in 40 rolls) he began betting that number every roll. When it failed to come up in another 30 rolls, he would double the size of his wager. Rarely did he fail to walk away with a profit.

Most of us don't have that kind of patience.

Mannie was a genius when it came to odds. One day he walked into a Las Vegas sports book establishment and looked at the odds board for the National League baseball teams making second place. He immediately made a $2,000 wager on *every* team. He had spotted a fallacy in the odds that were being offered. According to his mathematics, no matter which team won, he'd show a profit.

The house knew Mannie Kimmel. Immediately after they booked his bets, the odds were taken down, studied and changed.

In this case the bookies were right in making their change. Many times, however, when someone approaches the action in an unusual way, they become very concerned. They not only want to see what you're doing; they want to understand *why* you're doing it.

I'm reminded of this bit of gambling humor:

Asylum inmate to psychiatrist: "I'm a gambler."

Shrink: "Fine. You can gamble here."

"With whom?"

"Well, that fella over there is a bookie...."

"With what?"

"We use little stones from the driveway," said the shrink.

So the gambler went to the driveway, but instead of picking up pebbles he shouldered a boulder and carried it to the bookie.

"I want to make a bet with you," he said.

"Oh, no," said the bookie.

"Why not?" asked the gambler.

The bookie pointed to the boulder: "If you want to bet *that* big, you must *know* something!"

BACK TO serious business.

Watch this happen again and again at the table: A player will place a number. The number is thrown.

"Press it," he says. Most of his profits are added to the place bet.

It comes in again. "Press it," he says, again.

When it's all over he, too, walks away wondering why he has such poor luck.

What in the world was going through his mind? Even the greatest optimist among dice players doesn't fantasize about a hand in which the shooter will never ever again throw a seven!

Does the man who keeps saying "press it" and "press it" *really* want to win?

Think about it.

A POSTSCRIPT about that old-fashioned gambling hall, the Horseshoe. From 10 P.M. until 5:45 A.M. they'll serve you a 10-ounce steak as part of a complete dinner for $2.

Las Vegas is a value-oriented city.

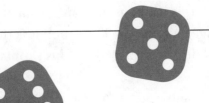

24

TOSSING THE DICE

M ost of today's craps shooters don't know all the rules, odds, betting procedures and other nuances. They're not that difficult to learn.

I often approach the dice table with a personal idiosyncrasy. I know that I don't have any more control of the little cubes than the next fellow, except that I never pick them up so that the numbers on top *or on the side facing me* are numbers that add up to a point I don't want.

I toss the dice. I take the fullest odds allowed behind my line bet. If I am flush with casino winnings or feeling very positive about things, I may not only make a "come" bet with three units, but I may put (place) $300 on each of the other numbers.

I buy rather than place the 4 and 10—paying the 5 percent vig ($15) on $300—and place the others. It doesn't pay to buy the others but it does to buy the 4 and 10. "Buying" means that if that number is thrown before a seven, I will receive the *true* 2-to-1 odds on my bet rather than 9-to-5.

BACK TO MY action. When I'm betting with the shooter, I want the dice to keep coming up 4, 5, 6, 8, 9, and 10..

When a number is thrown, I call "down with odds."

That means that my place (or buy) bet is paid off and the original bet and the profits are given to me except for the amount of money necessary to get full odds on my "come" bet, which is now moved to the same number. Now I make a new "come" bet.

Let's take the example of "10" which I have covered with a $300 "buy" bet, and paid $15 to buy it. A "10" is thrown. I'm paid off at the rate of 2-to-1. $600 for my $300.

My $300 "come" bet is moved to the 10 box and the dealer keeps $300 for full odds. Of the remaining $600, I rack up $300 and put $300 more on "come." If 10 comes in again, there is an "on-and-off" action in theory only, because none of the chips is actually moved. "Come" money to the 10 box and odds on the bet. And I am paid 9 units ($900).

6 or 8 pays even money on the first chip and 6-to-5 on the others for a payoff of 7-to-6. True odds are 6-to-5. 5 or 9 pays even money for the first chip and 3-to-2 on the others for a payoff of 7-to-5. True odds are 7-1/2-to-5. If you place 4 or 10 you get even money for the first chip and 2-to-1 on the others for a payoff of 9-to-5. True odds are 2-to-1. House percentages are 1.51 on 6 or 8; 4 percent on 5 or 9 and 6.68 on 4 or 10. Thus, it makes sense to place the 5, 6, 8 and 9, but to pay 4 percent to buy true odds on the 4 and 10.

Some casinos give the bettor an extra advantage. For example at the Horseshoe, the 5 percent vig is collected only if the wager wins.

DO I STAY with this forever?

No. I'm a skeptic. I don't believe Rabbi Schneerson was the Messiah, or that the Pope is infallible, or that there is such a thing as the Eternal Dice Hand where no "7" ever appears.

If I do well, at some point I make a decision to clean the board. I can, if I feel uneasy, call my odds money down at any time, and then just worry about the money that went from the "come" box to the numbers.

Or I can simply pick up my last "come" bet so there is nothing on "come." Then, as each number is rolled again, I am paid proceeds from the "come-went-to-a-number" wager and the accompanying odds bet.

You learned from your own home education course in tossing dice that those 7s are inevitable. At some point you want to gather as much money into your hands as possible before the dice show a seven.

REMEMBER THAT scene at Playboy when I called "odds working"?

The house rule is that odds are off on the come-out roll unless you declare otherwise. I thought long and hard about that one. I had a theory, and I wanted to find a fallacy in it. I couldn't. If having odds on a number is a good bet for the second roll, why isn't it also a good bet on the come-out roll?

Superstition. Shooters hate to roll a 7 on the come-out and then see all their "come" bets *and* that odds money get taken away by the dealer—even while the shooter wins his pass line bet.

So what? Is it any less painful if he rolls a 7 on the second roll when the odds *are* working?

My own instinct (with rare belly-hunch exceptions) is to announce that "My odds work all the time."

I win some, and I lose some. It hasn't been a bad bet at all. The reason the casino is content with the rule that odds are off on the come-out roll is that the odds bets are not profitable, so why encourage them?

Incidentally, if the house won't lose money on a true odds bet, why don't they all allow you triple or even unlimited true odds behind your line bet?

The answer is easy. If they allow you triple odds, you tend to bet less money on the line (where the house has a 1.41 percentage against you) and more money on true odds where the house has no advantage at all.

I happen to be very conscious of which numbers do and don't show up. For example, if I have placed or bought all the numbers and, by the time I 7-out, everything but the 9 has come in at least once, I'm likely to place the 9 after the next shooter throws a point. If it doesn't show up with him, I'll increase my wager.

Probability says that 9 should come up. We also know that it's possible that one won't come up for a half-hour. Unlikely, but possible.

Assuming a normal run of numbers, I consider it a good bet.

I'm also conscious of 7s. When a large number of 7s have come up in a short time, I remember when I tossed dice 144 times against my pillow at home. 7 is only supposed to come up once in six rolls. If there have been six 7s in fifteen rolls, it could mean that somebody may be about to throw a spate of numbers before another 7 shows its evil face.

Remember, too, that the improbable does happen. I watched a player throw eight consecutive craps. I also watched another throw six 4s in a row.

25

WAR STORIES FROM THE

GREEN FELT TABLES

It's mid-morning on a holiday weekend. The joint is jumping. The fellow to my right is playing with $500 (white) chips. He bets eight chips ($4,000) on "Don't" and then lays full odds after any number is thrown.

Obviously the casino has given him special limits because he has as much as $10,000 going against the shooter making his point.

I watch him win hand after hand.

The dice come to him and he waves them on, and the dice come to me.

"Be careful," I tell him. "I sometimes shoot a powerful hand."

He smiles.

I roll a number. Then lots of other numbers, but never the point.

He wins against me, too.

There aren't many players at the table. Twice more the dice come around and twice more I can't make a single point.

The fellow to my right is now winning more than $90,000.

Nobody asks, but I remark: "Were I you, I'd catch the next plane home."

He smiles enigmatically. No comment.

I leave.

Hours later I pass the table. He's still at it. His beard has begun to grow in. He appears weary. The pile of white chips in front of him is smaller.

Hours later he's still there. He's grim. And an obvious loser.

He should have been on that plane!

One of my lifetime friends, Allan J. Wilson, (not related to Allan N. Wilson the author) tells a happier tale. He was on a junket plane from New York to Las Vegas and happened to get into a conversation with a Chinese couple sitting next to him. In the course of the flight, he learned that they were unmarried, had been traveling companions for several years, and were in the export business.

They said they spent their holidays on trips to Las Vegas, the Bahamas, Puerto Rico and wherever else the Goddess of Chance beckoned. Although they acknowledged their share of gaming disasters, they insisted that their betting batting average had been good.

Later, in the casino, Allan found himself at the dice table shoulder to shoulder with the Chinese couple. They were "fooling around"—making small wagers, taking full odds on line bets and then full odds on their come bets.

Allan went his merry way to another casino. When he returned at midnight a pit boss he knew told him about the Chinese couple. According to the pit boss, they'd had a staggering winning run. They'd pyramided their modest bets into a $154,000 profit.

"What surprised me," said Allan, "was the couple's discipline. They'd cashed in their chips, checked out of the hotel and boarded the last plane of the night for San Francisco, where they planned to enjoy the balance of their holiday."

ALLAN AND I HAVE been together in many casinos. Years ago my first wife, Mary Louise, and I left him at a blackjack table at the Colony Club in London, where the chips bore George Raft's picture and where the only other player at the table at that time was the late Telly Savalas.

We returned at 2 A.M. The casino was almost empty. Allan stood at the dice table again with just one other player.

"How are you doing?" we asked.

"They've taken me to the cleaners," he said mournfully. "They've buried me."

"How much?"

"Twenty-five hundred dollars' worth."

We watched a few rolls of the dice and Mary Louise and I became simultaneously aware that Allan was doing something very wrong. *He wasn't taking odds!*

We joined the game, alternately lecturing him and sometimes forcefully grabbing chips from his rack to bet for him when he protested against putting down full odds.

He threw dice and we threw dice. The moment we took our eyes off him he tended to reduce or omit the odds bet. Again our lecture and the grappling for his chips. Within an hour he'd won back his losses and was $1,500 ahead.

I like to think we taught him how to bet at the crap tables.

When we returned to New York, Allan gifted us with some of the finest Zabar's caviar his winnings could buy!

ALLAN LIKES TO play and stay. I tell him that this means he must be a loser most of the time. He'll confess nothing, but he doesn't put up much argument.

Once, because he had no alternative, he *had* to hit-and-run. It happened at Del Webb's Sahara in Las Vegas. He happened not to like that hotel. He didn't like its restaurants and he had a consistent record of losing in the hotel's casino.

This time, however, he had no choice. His lady friend was insistent on seeing Johnny Carson, then starring in the Sahara showroom. Allan said he had seen enough Johnny Carson for two lifetimes, but the lady in his life wanted to see "if Johnny is as cute and charming" off the TV screen as he seemed to be on it.

It's tough to argue with a determined woman.

The couple arrived at the Sahara at 11:30 P.M.—half an hour before show time. Normally he would have been content to sit at a table and sip wine but Allan couldn't bring himself to pass a dice table that was almost deserted. There were two players in action and Allan figured both of them to be shills.*

The shooter had a one dollar chip on the pass line. He rolled an 11.

---

*He was probably wrong. Although Fremont Street casinos use shills to get a dice game started, Strip casinos usually do not use shills except at the baccarat tables.

"Seven has to come after 11," Allan told himself. It doesn't, but it did.

Then the shooter began to make numbers and Allan was betting on him all the way. At ten minutes to twelve, Allan's companion tugged at his sleeve. "Well miss the show," she complained. "We'll miss Johnny Carson."

He cashed in. Because *he had to* and was being dragged away.

Profits for the twenty minutes: $6,600.

"Johnny Carson was funnier than I can ever recall him being before," Allan J. Wilson told me.

ALLAN IS RESPONSIBLE for this amusing report. Being a sucker for gourmet-style restaurants, he liked to frequent the Sands in its heyday so he could dine at its Regency Room.

He was in the Sands casino one morning at 3 A.M. after a hearty dinner and show. The dice table was crowded and two wrong bettors were having the best of it.

You know the pattern. The shooter throws a number. His point is 9. He tosses two other numbers and then the inevitable cry from the stickman, "Out seven—a loser."

Allan watched the action for ten minutes without risking a *sou*. He was waiting for the dice to get to him. His expectation of being the next shooter was aborted when a scholarly-looking gentleman suddenly stepped up to the table to his right.

He apologized and asked if Allan minded if he picked up the dice first.

Impatient, Allan discarded his resolve not to bet until he held the dice. He bet "Don't pass." The man's first roll was a 7. Allan bet "Don't" again and the man threw another 7.

It was very disconcerting. Then came that infinite moment in time which all gamblers experience.

Let Allan tell it in his own words from here on: "Call it intuition, prescience, *déjà vu,* or what have you. I just *knew* this man was about to have a great roll. I put my chips on the line. He rolled an 8. Not a bad point. I took full odds behind the line, placed all the other numbers and made a come bet.

"Believe it or not, the shooter held the dice for thirty-eight minutes. He defied every law of probability. He didn't seem to be able to throw his 8 but he didn't throw another 7 either. He just kept tossing number after number after number.

"Most of us stood there not quite believing what we were witnessing.

"Suddenly the dice came up 8, the point. A loud cheer went up, for by now everyone around the table had gotten onto the roll and the cage was sending out tray after tray of additional chips.

"Now the shooter threw three craps in succession.

"My intuition again stood me in good stead. I took down everything that I could take down. He threw a 5 and then sevened out.

"Starting with a few hundred dollars, I had worked up a stake of just under $7,000.

"The shooter had done just about the same.

"The pit boss said to him, 'You should have won a hundred thou with a roll like that!'

"The fellow merely smiled and said, "I didn't want to hurt you.""

MENTION OF THE Regency restaurant at the Sands reminds me of an incident that illustrates how far a casino will go for a high roller.

One Saturday night my wife and I invited a friend, Mickey Leffert and his daughter Cheri, to join us. At 8 o'clock we walked into the Regency.

The maitre d' greeted me cordially.

"A table for four," I said.

"Mr. S., you didn't make a reservation."

"I never make a reservation," I said.

"You should have," he said, expressing dismay. "It's Saturday night, I don't have anything until ten o'clock."

I left my group standing there and went to the casino shift boss and told him my problem. He raced into the Regency in double-time. "Why aren't you giving Mr. S. a table?" he said, challengingly.

"I don't have one," he said.

"What about that one?" the shift boss said, pointing to an empty.

"That's reserved for Dean Martin."

"What about that one?" he said, pointing to a second empty table.

"That's reserved for Mr. Davis." (Chester Davis was currently in charge of the Hughes casinos.)

The shift boss stomped out with me at his side, grumbling about how the casino used to run the hotel but now—.

While I hurried to the office of Charles Turner, one of the owners, the maitre d' was telling my wife, "Mrs. Stuart, you know there's no one we'd rather seat than you and your husband. But if I gave you either of those tables, I'd be fired before you could sit down."

I walked into Turner's office without knocking. "Charley, can't I get a table in the Regency?"

"What are you talking about?" he said. I explained and then had to run to keep up with him as he charged into the restaurant.

He repeated the shift boss's questions about "Whose table is that?" for each of the two empties. When told, he understood quickly. No explanation was needed.

Charley surveyed the room. He pointed to a desirable booth. "Who is sitting there?" he asked. The maitre d' consulted his reservation card.

"That's Mr. and Mrs. Arthur Milton."

"Who's sitting at that table?" Charley asked, pointing to another.

Again the maitre d' consulted his card. "That's Mr. & Mrs. John Johnson."

"Put em together," Charley ordered. "Then give Mr. Stuart and his guests the empty."

"But Mr. Turner, the Miltons and the Johnsons don't know each other!"

Charley winked at me. For him the problem was solved. "They'll know each other by the time they've finished eating," he said, as he turned to leave.

My guests were very impressed.

26

THE SOLID GOLD DICE

Casino craps are called "bank craps" because the casino banks the game and you can bet with or against the shooter.

In times past, dice or "the cubes" were made from such sources as rock crystal, marble, woodchuck, deer teeth, and buffalo bones.

A pair of dice may cost you $20,000 for an unlucky session at the tables but they cost the casino less than $2. Casino dice are sawed from cellulose rods and are manufactured to an accuracy of 1/10,000th of an inch. This is about 1/20th of the thickness of a human hair. When I was a tentative point-holder in the Aladdin, one of its casino executives, Jimmy Konys, would sometimes present a heavy loser at the dice table with a pair of dice with the player's name printed on them in gold.

The owner of these dice invariably went home, showed them around, and boasted that he'd received them because "I rolled such a long hand."

Perhaps if he told the story often enough he would believe it himself. And remember, Konys gave the gold dice *only* to losers!

RECENTLY THE GRAND (Bally's) in Atlantic City gave one of its high rollers a gift of solid gold dice. They cost the casino $8,000.

I met the gold dice recipient on a junket. He may drop as much as one million dollars a year at craps so what else do you give a guy who can lose a million a year but solid gold dice?

The high roller junket is a type the average comp-hungry player doesn't even dream about. And it marks a different direction insofar as junkets are concerned.

In the old days a junket brought "good players" to the casinos and kept them there. Today the casinos are on a different tack.

Here's a junket Carole and I went on several months ago. It was limited to six couples. We started with a private dinner at The Grand, attended by Bally's President, Arthur Goldberg. Then we were escorted to the best seats in the showroom for a performance by Liza Minnelli.

The next day separate limousines drove each couple from Atlantic City to the Philadelphia airport where we flew, First Class, to Phoenix, Arizona. What amused me was that the limo seat across from us was stocked with a selection of bagels, lox, cheeses, Danish pastry, coffee, milk, etc.

In Phoenix, a fleet of limousines met us at the airport to drive us to the Phoenician in Scottsdale. This resort was built with a billion or so dollars of taxpayer money, stolen from the public by that wretched parody of a human being, Charles Keating.

Keating pretended to be virtuous (he led an anti-pornography organization) and generous, even while stealing the life-savings of thousands of elderly couples. To his credit, the place is beautiful beyond description. At least the creep had good taste in designing resorts!

Carole and I joked about none of the well-trained staff being over the age of 22.

We were given a lovely suite. Meals were excellent and some evenings the limousine took us to the best restaurants with our Bally hostess Wendy Vogt. On other occasions, we were taken on tours. Carole was gifted with several hundred dollars worth of credit in the hotel shops.

After a week, it was back to the east where waiting limos would whisk us to our homes.

(In our case, I cut our vacation short by a day so I could fly back to Atlantic City for their baccarat tournament. I won it—but more of that later.)

The cost of this junket to the casino was $60,000—or $10,000 a couple.

Generous? Yes, and then again, no. Rather, very smart. Any of the six players could easily drop the total cost of the junket in one sit-down in the casino. The goal for the casino is to develop loyalty out of gratitude.

ATLANTIC CITY CASINOS have offered to Concorde Carole and me to Paris and put us up at a luxury hotel for a week, dining us in three-star restaurants, etc. They've offered us a cruise on the *Sea Goddess*. They've offered us a trip to Portugal at Donald Trump's expense. They've offered us the best seats at the World Cup soccer finals and front row center seats for the Three Tenors concert in Hollywood.

This year I decided to accumulate casino invitations and promotion pieces instead of tossing them into the waste basket. In the first six months, I collected a carton-full that weighs more than twelve pounds!

SOME YEARS AGO I knew a fellow whom I'll call Billy G. Billy was a successful owner of retail gift shops in Phoenix, Arizona including one at the airport. He had a lovely wife.

Billy was a dice degenerate. He went for his cash. He went for his checks. He went for his markers. He went for his last buck. He went very broke.

His wife divorced him.

One day he sat in a plane at the Cleveland airport waiting for the plane to take off. The plane exploded on the runway and sixty people were killed. Eight passengers in the rear section (including an infant) were blown safely out of the plane and Billy was one of the lucky eight. Billy vowed never to set foot in an plane again.

To get to Las Vegas from Phoenix by train or automobile is quite a trip. Billy made it frequently.

One day at a casino called The Royal Nevadan, Billy got lucky at the crap tables. When he was ready to cash in, he was an $80,000 winner.

There was consternation in the cashier's cage and an interminable delay as he stood around impatiently waiting to receive his eighty grand.

Finally he was ushered into the executive offices. "Mr. G.," he was told, "We're embarrassed to tell you that at this moment we don't have enough cash in the cage to pay you off. Maybe there's something else we can work out."

After much conversation, Billy, was offered two shops in the hotel arcade rent-free for eighteen months. He said he'd think about it and went home with a receipt for the $80,000. Then he sent his accountant to Las Vegas.

The accountant arrived and the casino opened its books and records for him. "The place can't last, Billy," he reported. "Certainly not for eighteen months."

Billy G. thought about it. "Well, something is better than nothing," he announced, and accepted the offer.

Six months passed and Billy recouped his eighty thousand, and then some, from sales in the two shops. Then he received an "urgent" summons to Las Vegas.

He made the long journey. Once again he was ushered into the executive offices. "Billy, you've got an interest in this place so I thought I should tell you that we're probably going to go belly-up in about ten days."

Twenty thousand dollars in Royal Nevadan chips were pushed toward him.

"Take these. Spread em around town. Do it quickly."

In those days , the chips of any casino were cashable at every other casino in town. Banks and merchants accepted them as money and made change for them—usually in silver dollars.

Billy spread the chips around by using them at other casino dice tables. He did okay for himself.

A week later The Royal Nevadan closed its doors. Its chips were worthless and those who held them were stuck with them.

Years have passed. Billy still makes the tiresome railroad journey to Las Vegas. Still plays Bank Craps. Still is a constant loser.

MOST LOSERS PAY their debts. Less than 4 percent of all credit extended by Nevada casinos is uncollected. This, despite the fact that a large percentage of the income of some casinos is based on credit. (The I.R.S. does not require the casino to consider winnings as income until they've been collected.)

Credit investigation systems are quite sophisticated. Take, for example, the Las Vegas Hilton. A file is kept of all persons who ever requested credit. The customer's card contains such information as his junket history, whether his markers are paid at the tables, the cage, or whether he leaves town owing money. In addition to showing his credit limit, the card rates him as a player. Many players are rated by two supervisors in the pit every time they play.

At Caesars Palace, where as much as 50 percent of the play used to depend on credit, credit markers consist of four sheets of paper which are divided into six stubs each. At any time it is possible to account for all the markers. A computer system monitors 70,000 active credit cards and another 50,000 inactive ones. The casino is plugged into the Central Credit Bureau so that it can monitor your action, credit line, and money owed at other casinos in town.

A MIDDLE-AGED FELLOW with a mustache walked up to the dice table. His accent marked him Hispanic. I watched him drop four white ($500) chips onto the field—one of the worst wagers on the casino craps layout.*

The field bet is a sucker's bet and is often called a "ladies' bet" because it appeals to the novice with that nice big space that pays off when the shooter rolls any one of those seven numbers. The selection is usually 2, 3, 4, 9, 10, 11 or 12. Even with a 2-to-1 payoff on 2 and 12, you will win 18 chips and lose 20 chips if you bet a chip on every roll.

So here, before my very eyes, was a man betting $2,000 on one of the worst bets on the table.

What followed was a series of 2s and 12s and 3s and 9s and 11s. Within minutes he was $20,000 ahead.

"It owes me this," he said. "They really put it to me at baccarat last night!"

The dice came around to me. I wished to myself that he would quit. He didn't. I threw a 6. Then an 8. Then I sevened-out. Cost to him: $6,000.

He continued to make only field bets. I moved away. I didn't want to witness the massacre.

If you've been at enough tables, you've seen it in variation. An improbable series of lucky wins. But the player has no goals, no discipline, no ability to quit a winner. Soon he'll quit losers.

Don't let it be you.

---

*The house has an advantage ranging from 5.263 percent to 11.111 percent depending on whether or not it offers a double payoff on 2 or 12. That's not as bad as proposition bets like 2, 3, 11 or 12—all of which give the house 16.866 percent.

27

MORE DICE ADVICE

Mannie Kimmel used to insist to me that results would be the same if a monkey threw the dice.

If, however, you take an intense dislike to the guy at the other end because he appears to be an anal character smoking a smelly cigar, my advice is to stand aside and not bet. You'll not be happy betting with him. And if you are suckered by your emotions into betting against him, you're playing temperamental dice and losing control and perspective.

On the other hand, occasionally you'll see someone pick up the dice and you'll have a strong positive feeling. It's worth taking a larger than usual chance. Play hunches. There's nothing wrong with it. You'll be right often and wrong often.

I have played some far-out hunches when I held the dice. For example, I will occasionally make a proposition bet that isn't even on the table. It's called "a hopping bet" and is available in Nevada but not in New Jersey. It is a stupid, odds-against-me bet. I call a number in exactly the way I believe it will fall. Thus, I don't say "6" but rather "4 and 2 on the hop."

It's a one-roll wager, and I lose if any other number comes up or even if "6" comes up any other way.

Some years ago when *Life* published its rather silly article about me, they included two paragraphs about my gambling, which read:

> Back at the crap tables, the dice came to Stuart and something eerie happened. He began to glow. Call it a hallucination, a trick played by the casino lights—I saw it and so did the man standing next to me. Stuart suddenly began to glow like a filament charged with current. He was going to have a streak. The pit boss appeared quickly from nowhere. "A Lyle Stuart streak," he told me later, "is one of the spectacles of gambling. In five minutes, counting side bets, he can take the house for a hundred grand."
>
> Stuart can't explain how it happens.
>
> All he knows is that for four or five minutes he knows exactly what the dice or cards are going to do. He stared at the dice now, bright red against the dark green table. Patted them, smacked them, fussed with them as a mother fusses with a baby. Suddenly he snapped them up and flung them the length of the table. "5 and 2!" he yelled while the dice were still in the air; 5 and 2 came up.
>
> The whole table gasped. Once more Stuart fidgeted with the dice and then flung them. "Hard 6!" he yelled. Two 3s showed. The table was in an

uproar. Next, he called 11 and made it. Then 4. Then 9. The crowd stood three deep.

Men were yelling, women squealing. Dealers were paying bets as fast as their hands could move. In five minutes he won $31,000.

AS WITH MOST of the rest of the article, it was bullshit. But it brings up the subject of precognition and ESP.

Do I believe in any god or gods or supernatural destiny? No. I'm an atheist from way back.

If you believe there is some god or gods watching over you, more power to you and your imagination. From Thomas Edison to Albert Einstein, the most knowledgeable scientists of our time—and those who best understood how the universe works—discarded the idea of a personal deity.

So you still believe this giant IBM machine in the sky is going to look down on you (among its five billion subjects) and care whether your dice turn up a 6 or 7?

Good for you.

I tend to go along with crusading journalist George Seldes in that I believe nothing I hear and only half of what I see. (A few days before I wrote this, George celebrated his 104th birthday.)

I don't know the explanations for everything, but I do know that there *are* explanations. I don't believe human beings are at the top of the mountain in learning about things that happen on the earth on whose crust we live.

With that as prelude, let me say that it is only at gambling that my senses have been so acute on occasion that I have had what others might label mystical experiences.

Nothing supernatural, but flashes for which I do not yet have the explanation.

Let's backtrack for a moment. If you are of my generation, you're familiar with the Rodgers and Hart song "Where or When," in which "some things that happen for the first time, seem to be happening again."

We've all felt that feeling. It's called *déjà vu*. We've also all had hunches. And when the hunches came true on some occasions the results chilled us.

As regards gaming, you stand at a table and you feel the next roll of the dice will be an 8 or a 7 or an 11—whatever. And it *happens that way!* Wow! It's very vivid and you recall it for the rest of the day and the day after, too.

What you don't remember...what you tend to immediately white out of your memory are those hunches that *don't* come true. The man or lady picks up the dice. "Oh, oh," you tell yourself, "it's gonna be 7-out."

The next roll is a 10. You completely forget *that* hunch.

Being aware of this and of the occasional (sometimes only once in four days, sometimes four times in two days) streaks of foreknowledge I believed I had, I decided to test myself to put to rest once and for all this peculiar feeling that my mind somehow was racing ahead of time.

To check me out, I had my friend Morris Sorkin accompany me to a casino. When I got those premonitions, I announced it to him in a quiet voice. I didn't merely say "8" , but rather "5 and 3." Not just 4 but "3 and 1."

The feeling came upon me the second day. I *called eleven consecutive rolls of the dice exactly right!* On the twelfth roll I said "two aces" and the dice rolled a 2 and a 1. Close, yes?

I HAVE HAD similar (though not as extended) experiences at baccarat. I've known exactly what my cards were before turning them over. On one occasion (when I was dealing from the shoe) the Player side showed an 8.

"That's okay," I announced with complete confidence, "I've got a 2 and a 7." And that's what I turned over.

I'd then call the next few cards dealt to Player and to Bank exactly right.

It has worked in reverse, too. Betting on Player, I've turned over an 8, and when someone nearby remarked, "Good," I've replied, "No good. The bank has a 9."

And indeed it did.

Are there explanations? Of course. I'm not a magician or a mentalist. I'm neither a sage nor a clairvoyant. But this thing at the dice table has happened to me often. (Once, when somebody's dice were in the air I shouted "$100 on aces!" and the box man yelled "Bet!" and aces they were. This caused actor-producer Sidney Poitier, who was at my side, to grab my arm and say, "You've got to tell me how you play this game!" even while the croupier was counting out the $3,000 payoff for my hunch call.

I've speculated that perhaps I've been standing at dice tables so long over a forty-five-year period that my mind has become a computer with some anticipation of what should come up because it hasn't come up.

I don't know. When it happens, I don't fight it: I go with it.

DO YOU REMEMBER poker player's lament Kenny Rogers sang, "Know When to Hold em and Know When to

Fold em", or song lyricist Hal David's "Knowing When To Leave"?

If you're tired, walk away. If the smoke from some-body's cigarette bothers you, walk away. (Ask for a non-smoking table. Most casinos now have them and if enough players ask for them, eventually the management or the law will ban all smoking in casinos. (The MGM Grand started with thirty percent of its rooms as non-smoking rooms and has increased this to fifty percent.)

If you feel unlucky, walk away.

If the stickman moves too quickly for your peace of mind, walk away.

If *anything* at all bothers you, walk away.

Walking away is one of the smartest moves you can make in a casino.

The dice game is as eternal as anything can be in our lifetime. It doesn't end when you walk away. It doesn't begin when you place your first wager.

It's going on all the time. Every day and every night of the year. Now. Even at this moment. Even while you read this sentence, dice are rolling on hundreds upon hundreds of green felt tables, and thousands upon thousands of dol-lars are being won and lost.

Don't panic or feel any great sense of loss. You're not losing your last opportunity when you walk away

The game goes on forever. It will go on after you and I are dead, buried and forgotten.

There's plenty of time to resume your action.

Relax.

28

THE PATIENT MAN'S
DICE SYSTEM

In the beginning I told you what I believe about systems.

Dictionary definition? System: A whole composed of parts in orderly arrangement according to some scheme or plan; the set of correlated principles, ideas, or statements belonging to some department of knowledge or belief.

Gamble: Any course involving risk and uncertainty.

Dictionary definitions would seem to make the two words, "gambling" and "system," incompatible if not mutually exclusive. Yet gambling systems have existed for centuries.

There is no honest "system" that will consistently overcome casino odds. But just to show you one of the paradoxes in gambling, I'll let you in on a "system" given to me by one of the biggest gamblers of our time. (The only thing I won't reveal here is his name.)

Years ago Irving Caesar (he wrote the lyrics for "Tea for Two"; "Swanee"; "I Want To Be Happy") brought us together because Irving wanted Mr. Gambling Man to dissuade me from gambling.

The three of us spent a pleasant evening in conversation and now we were sitting in a fancy restaurant that was obviously ("secretly") owned by Mr. Gambling Man.

He told me nothing I didn't know. How gamblers are idiots. How they're every kind of fool. How they're self-destructive clowns, etc., etc., etc.

I frustrated his sermonizing by agreeing completely. At about 2 A.M. a twinkle appeared in his blue eyes. "I'll demonstrate to you what assholes gamblers are," he said. "Take you. You say you like craps. Would you risk $2,700 to win $25?"

"Repeat that?" I said.

He did.

"Do you think I'm crazy?" I said.

"Of course! Now listen to me. This is the wager. You're going to bet that four consecutive players at the dice table won't each make at least four passes. Once in a long long while you'll get unlucky and you'll lose. But generally, you're gonna do fine. Interested?"

I nodded, albeit reluctantly.

He explained the "system."

I published the details in my first gaming book and it brought me more mail and phone calls than anything else in its pages.

It consists of a series of wagers. You bet on the "Don't pass" side. You bet $25. If the shooter makes a pass, you bet $50. Then $100. Then $200.

If anywhere along the line he misses, you've made $25. If he makes four passes, you stand back and wish him luck and hope he makes 100 passes: they don't affect you. You don't wager again until the dice are passed to the next shooter. Then you begin with a new sequence: $50, $75,

$150 and $300. If that shooter makes four passes, you wait until the dice move to the next shooter. Then the sequence is $75, $100, $200 and $400. The fourth and final sequence is $100, $125, $250 and $500.

As soon as you win a bet you go back to the first sequence.

If four players in a row make four passes or more each, you have lost $2,700.

The odds against it happening are heavy, though I wasn't convinced of that the first time I flew to Las Vegas with the "system" and approached the table with trepidation.

Moving from table to table (I'd move when I'd won $300 to $400 at a table) I found myself with $2,800 in winnings in about two hours.

I kept playing this little number on subsequent visits.

Sometimes as many as three shooters would make four or more passes each and then it was a while before I got even again. But even I got.

There are two pitfalls to the bet.

One is that sometime, and probably when you can least afford it, you're going to lose $2,700. It didn't happen to me but it could have happened and it could happen.

The other and more critical (to me) negative is that it is the dullest way to spend time in a casino that you can possibly imagine. You are a machine, bored silly for hours while you wait for outcomes that may take fifteen rolls each before you win or lose $25.

Another factor that affects some people is reluctance to play on the "Don't pass" side because they're afraid that people at the table will dislike them.

You're not in the casino to win popularity contests. You aren't playing against the shooter. You're playing against the house. But that isn't enough for some sensitive souls. If playing "Don't" makes you that uncomfortable, then *don't*.

A comment that, I hope, will save me countless additional phone calls and postage stamps. "What happens if I'm on the third sequence with my first bet of $75 and I win it? Do I go back to a first bet of $25?"

I deliberately left my original explanation vague because there is no easy answer. You can go back to $25. Or, if you're losing money in this contest, you can stay with $75 for a few hands—because if a few shooters don't make their first passes, you recover money at the rate of $75 a clip instead of $25.

Readers also wrote to ask why they should increase the first bet to $50, then $75 and $100, thus greatly enlarging the amounts of the subsequent bets in each sequence.

The reason is that since each new player has only a 50-50 chance of making a pass, you recover your loss more quickly. However, the fact is that you can stick to the $25, $50, $100, and $200 sequence for all four players and thus risk only $1,000 instead of $2,700.

All clear?

I ONCE EXPLAINED this "system" to a friend of mine. Then I watched him at the table. Whenever the results were going against him, requiring a bet of $400, he chickened out. He'd stand there without making the bet. Ironically, again and again on that non-wager, the player would 7-out. Or come out with craps. (Keep in mind that only "2" or "3" pay off on the "Don't" side since, to give the house its advantage, "12 is a push"—you neither win nor lose.)

Need I add that on his return from any gambling journey the question is never did he win, but rather how much did he lose?

29

ABSENT THEE FROM FELICITY AWHILE

Charles Kandel was a delightful fellow to know. Everyone liked him. He was warm, gracious and generous.

In the old days Charley, whose nickname was "Toolie" for reasons you probably can imagine, sat to the left of Arnold Rothstein ("The Big Bankroll") at the front table in the old Lindy's restaurant, the smaller one on the east side of Broadway that was run by Mrs. Leo Lindy.

Jack "Legs" Diamond sat on Rothstein's right. Kandel and Diamond were Rothstein's collectors.

Rothstein was, among other nefarious things, a loan shark. He was a "6-for-5" man. You borrowed $5 for one week and paid back $6. That's slightly more than 1,000 percent annual interest. Better than they'll pay you at Chase Manhattan Bank.

The borrower would look into Rothstein's steel blue eyes and say, "Arnold, I'll have this back to you within a month," and Rothstein would reply, "God help you if you don't." And there he was, surrounded by those grim-looking collectors.

Rothstein invented the inter-city "layoff" system that insured bookmakers against disastrous losses. This marked the beginning of a nationwide illegal gambling apparatus. He was also adept at fixing sporting events. But his claim to notoriety was the introduction of organization to the illegal gambling profession.

World War I and something new called the income tax failed to dampen America's gambling fever. Rothstein prospered. In 1919, he established a luxurious illegal gambling house in Saratoga, New York. He was able to "juice" it into protection by making big bribes to the Saratoga police.

His criminal career was not limited to gambling interests. He took advantage of the business potential created by Prohibition. He financed retail outlets for bootleggers and provided them with trucks and drivers. He also operated a large bail bond and insurance business.

Rothstein's addiction to gambling eventually cost him his life. He was shot in the groin during a dispute in a poker game in 1928 at what was then called the Park Central Hotel. He died a few days later from complications. He refused to identify his killer to the police.

IN CLEVELAND, Moe Dalitz was a bootlegger and top mobster but in Vegas he became the elder statesman of the gaming industry and was thought of as a very nice fellow. In Detroit, Eddie Levinson paid $1,500 in fines for running an illegal sawdust joint. In Las Vegas he became a wealthy captain of the industry. And so it went.

Those were the old days. The days when the mustaches found there was more money in legal gambling than in extortion and hijacking. The days when they all became gentlemen and churchmen and heads of the local charities.

When it became necessary to gun down the father of it all, Benjamin "Bugsy" Siegel, the gunning-down was done in Beverly Hills.

When it became necessary, in 1958, to stab to death casino owner Gus Greenbaum and his wife, it was done with butcher knives in Arizona. He was almost decapitated.

The "boys" had become paragons of virtue. In their Las Vegas legal casinos, they recognized quickly something the Quakers had learned centuries before: honesty is the best policy.

There was no need to cheat at the games. The games were themselves a license to steal. There was no need to be anything but fine gentlemen.

Charley Kandel became a gentleman.

He set up a scholarship foundation. He was a veteran of more wars than you'd want to remember, and he was active in veteran affairs. Audie Murphy, the most decorated hero of World War II, was Charley's friend. So was Captain Ernest O. Medina, of My Lai massacre notoriety.

Charley worked at the Sands as a host. His brother was a Hollywood screenwriter. When Howard Hughes bought the Sands, Charles became "Casino Executive."

He greeted people.

People liked him. He had his own set of ethics and loyalties, and he was true to them. He knew every scam, every form of larceny, every kind of con.

Charley was a genuinely charming fellow. He also taught me a rule that I abandoned when I decided to write my first casino book.

"If you want to get rich, get rich in the dark."

IF YOU WANT TO GET RICH,
GET RICH IN THE DARK.

There are many reasons for this. There are those who feel that the I.R.S. doesn't play on a level playing field. You can't deduct casino losses, but you are supposed to pay taxes on winnings. Some gamblers consider this rule so unfair they don't.

But a reason to operate quietly is that casino operators are as superstitious as their customers. They become uncomfortable when you win and win and win. They may not want your business after a while. Remember that some of them still fire blackjack dealers who run "unlucky" and lose money for the casino.

There was one time when dealers were fired if they smiled the wrong way, said a wrong word or had Jewish-sounding names. This happened when builder Del Webb put a vice president of his construction company in charge of one of his casinos.

This vice president knew little about gaming but he loved the power and he hated Jews, Blacks and Hispanics. Nor was he shy about letting the world know his feelings.

This went on for a couple of days with dealers, croupiers and supervisors being fired arbitrarily and in nasty fashion.

This character was standing at a crap table when two men stepped on each side of him.

"Hi, Jimmy," one of them said.

He stared.

"Moe sent us." Jimmy knew they meant Moe Dalitz.

After a pause, the spokesman continued: "Moe says he hears you've been saying some nasty things about Jews."

There was another pause.

"Moe doesn't like it."

Another pause.

"Moe says if you make one more remark about Jews, we're to break your arms and legs."

The silence was deafening. Everyone around the dice table seemed to freeze.

"Moe says if you don't believe him, say something now."

The three-days-in-office casino manager didn't utter a word. His face turned pale as he hurried from the casino.

That night he left Las Vegas forever.

CASINO MANAGERS are superstitious.

They really believe that dice are "hot" or "cold."

Dice are man-made objects with no mind, no memory, no eyes, no nose, no mouth. The only time they become "hot" is when you roast them on a skillet over a lit stove. They can become "cold" if you put them in the freezing section of your refrigerator.

That casino personnel believe dice run "hot" and "cold" only proves that they're almost as crazy as you are for playing their odds-against-you games.

Here is my suggested method of operation that will separate the will-to-winners from the wish-to-winners.

GO TO CASINOS ALONE.

No wife. No girl friend. No companions.

You aren't there for fun and games. You don't want to play to play. You want to play to win. You're on a serious mission. If you don't want it to be "Mission Impossible," it will require all your concentration.

If you have company, your movements are restricted. You will be spending time in dining rooms and show rooms. You will be talking to your friend at the tables (and thus dissipating your energy and focus) or eyeing your watch to check when you meet again.

Don't.

And don't tell me about the time you were with a party of eight people and won a lot of money. It's possible. In games of chance, anything is possible.

30

G O L D E N   G U L C H

In 1993, Nevada casinos grossed nearly seven billion dollars. Las Vegas accounted for more than 75 percent of this figure—or $4.521 billion. And that ain't succotash.

In Atlantic City, nine casinos reported a gross win of $459,500,000. In December 1979, these nine averaged wins of about a half million dollars a day. In the latest figures before me, the Casino Association of New Jersey reports that its gaming halls raked in profits of $352,000,000. Atlantic City casinos do shear the gullibles as they arrive.

Keep in mind that Nevada had a fifty-year monopoly on the casino gaming industry.

The tax on casino earnings ranges from 3 to 6.25 percent. The casino doesn't pay it. The players do.

In one survey, one-third of the visitors polled said that gambling was the main reason they came to Nevada. About as many said the main attraction was the shows.

You shouldn't be interested in any of it.

The amusement park atmosphere is designed for the people who lose all that money that pays all those taxes. If you gamble, you are a person who reads more books, newspapers and magazines than the non-bettor. You watch less television, go to more nightclubs, and attend more movies and theaters.

Fine. But do those things in your hometown. You traveled to the casino to win.

Okay, why do I talk only in terms of American casinos? What about Monte Carlo? Macao?

Here I speak only for myself. I've gambled in many places, ranging from casinos in France, with $10,000 table limits, to Elsinore Castle in Denmark, where the limit was $2. (Copenhagen now has a large modern casino.)

I've gambled in Venice where I would win "a million" at a time. One chip. Lira, dammit—and worth, at the rate of less than 1,600 to an American dollar, only $625.

To overcome the casino advantage I find my best location is a city where I'm not locked into the casino. I want to be able to gamble at any hour of the day or night when I feel like gambling. I want to be able to move from table to table and from casino to casino on impulse.* I want to play where my winnings are not critical for the casino.

I also want to gamble only when I'm ready for it. I don't want the casino to be located three blocks from where I live. Gambling facilities that close would be dangerous for me. Going to gamble should require time and effort. A pilgrimage. Atlantic City, being less than two and one half

---

*I almost always rent a car because although taxis are plentiful and their cost reasonable, I want the pleasure of my own company and a chance to think and plan as I pick my next target.

hours away is more dangerous for me than Reno, Las Vegas or Carson City.

Proximity is dangerous. While only 61 percent of all adult Americans bet on anything, 78 percent of all Nevada residents bet on something.

Atlantic City has little to offer but the gambling. Its twelve casinos currently offer more than 13,000 25-cent slot machines; more than 3,300 50-cent machines; more than 5,000 dollar slots plus some 783 5-dollar machines.

Las Vegas has more than 7,000 nickel machines. Yes, *nickel* machines! It has 28,000 quarter slots (more than twice as many as Atlantic City) and more than 10,000 dollar slots (again, double what Atlantic City has).

Vegas also has lots of $25, $100 and $500 slots for those crazy enough to play them.

THE ATTEMPT TO turn a slum city like Atlantic City into a resort town would have taken a sultan's fortune, and there were no wandering sultans around. It's still Slum City. Las Vegas as an entertainment center casts a giant shadow over Hollywood—grossing more than the film industry and all the Disney playgrounds combined. The shrewd keepers of the Vegas casinos look upon Atlantic City as a school where more people will learn how to play casino games.

Gambling and crime are still linked in the public mind.

Tourists make easy targets for robbers, pickpockets, purse snatchers and burglars. One out of every five crime victims in Las Vegas is an out-of-state visitor. In Atlantic City at night, it isn't unusual for a gun to be put to your head when you exit the casino onto a dark street.

Just knowing this should alert you against carrying large sums of cash on your person when you're roaming the streets of any casino town. Nor is concealing it in the dirty laundry in your hotel room any protection. Hotel keys are like moments of depression: everybody has them.

Almost every new hotel now has a safe in every suite where you set your own code on the combination lock.

Studies have shown that gambling remains the heartbeat of organized crime, both locally and nationally.

Mob influence in casinos? Syndicate control became smaller over the years as large corporations took over casino after casino.

Let us assume that somehow the "boys" still have their hands in some of the tills. And some of the hands are hidden. (Caesars Palace was the last casino under the control of the "mustaches" and they're gone now.)

Wouldn't you like to become as lucky as Allen R. Glick? For $22,500 Glick bought a real estate company which happened to be worth $10,500,000.

That's a jackpot win if ever there was one.

Glick was such a nice fellow that the Teamsters Union Pension Fund loaned him almost $150,000,000 so that his company, Argent (French for money!), could own and control the Stardust, Fremont, Hacienda and Marina in Las Vegas.

What does any of this mean to you?

Nothing, if whatever happens behind the scenes doesn't pressure employees to cheat you. You need be concerned only with scams which involve cheating the players in order to make up for employee cheating.

Sure there are plenty of scam operations that involve dealers. Again, none of these is your problem. If you play in large casinos that have big bankrolls, your sole goal is to win.

Let the Feds worry about the mob influence.

In my first book I told about the behind-the-scenes activity at the Sands after the so-called mob disposed of its interest in the place. Two years later, the remaining partners had a falling out and the Sands was sold to Howard Hughes.

Cheap. A bargain. Nevertheless the selling price was so much more than "the boys" had received for their (hidden ownership) points, that word went to the new sellers: "Cut us a piece of your pie."

The request didn't come from Mafia muscle. Rather, it came from Frank Erickson, the gambler's layoff man.

Not a demand. Just a request.

Then Sandy Waterman, Charles Turner, Carl Cohen and the others decided to accommodate "the boys"—who, under the table, were given an additional $10,000 a point—or $1,000,000 as a bonus.

Now Howard Hughes was happy, the sellers were happy, and "the boys" were happy.

COMPS FOR ROOM, food, drinks, entertainment and air transportation cost the casino hotels a big portion of their operating budget.

If you are a heavy gambler, casinos are willing to spend 20 percent and sometimes as much as 32 percent of your line (the money they expect you to drop) to make you comfortable.

Of major concern these days are comp cheats: those people who work to get comps for which they don't really qualify. There are, for example, petty minds who focus on beating the casino out of complementaries by seeming to be bigger gamblers than they really are. Some fanatics break it down to a "science" by doing such weird things as figuring ways to slow down the number of deals at the blackjack table so that they're actually playing fewer hands than average at the table.

There was a time when junketeers drew chips against markers, played some and had someone else cash the rest. The markers were uncollectable. In some cases scam artists, using forged documents of identity got credit in the name of someone who was terminally ill.

Which reminds me. The casinos used to write off debts when an individual dies. No more. The courts recently ruled that a person's estate can be held accountable and the debt collectable.

YOU'RE GOING TO give them a chance at your money and they're going to give you a chance at theirs. But most of the chips are stacked on their side of the table and you don't owe them a thing.

You do owe yourself every opportunity to win their money and to keep it.

Winning, of course, is one thing. Keeping is another. We've agreed that you aren't a winner until you get your money home.

The mousetrap here is your unwillingness to leave town on the turn of a big win.

There are players who open local bank accounts.* Others buy bank checks and mail them home. Others hand the money to friends for safekeeping.

For years a running gag in the casino was the husband turning to his wife and saying, "Gimme that money I told you not to gimme."

You have to work out your own money-escape method. And then stick to it.

---

*If you deposit large amounts of cash in a bank you'll have to pay tax on it or show the I.R.S. that you've had equivalent losses. England takes a different view: no income tax is imposed on gambling winnings there.

The I.R.S. guidelines on gambling record-keeping would confound a rocket scientist. They want you to keep a diary showing the date and type of specific wagers. Name and address of the casino. Name(s) of person(s) if any who were there when you played. The amount(s) won or lost. The number of the dice table at which you played. Information as to whether credit was issued in the pit or at the cashier's cage. And so forth, ad infinitum.

31

I BREAK MY OWN RULES

I sometimes violate my own rules. Let me share a few anecdotes.

Jon Gilbert does a masterful job directing our publishing business. I brought him to his first casino and he loved it. Then I took a group of six employees to Atlantic City and gave each a chance to throw dice while I bet on their behalf. My wagering started with $75 on the pass line; full double odds behind it and then two $300 place bets and a $75 come bet.

If they didn't win money, I gave them a second chance. The bottom line is that I went home with six happy people who carried with them winnings that ranged from $650 to $4,200.

Jon was one of those winners and he was "hooked" on casino gambling.

So one sunny day I called an Atlantic City casino for a limo. (I have $100,000 credit lines at five of them, so a limousine is a modest request.)

I invited Jon to join me.

We arrived in A.C. before noon. The baccarat game was just being opened. Not wanting to be the sole player, I gave Jon some chips and invited him to sit down beside me.

Jon cut the cards.

I made a large bet on Bank, and he, a minimum wager on Player. I dealt to him from the shoe. He turned over a natural 9.

He took the shoe. I made a large bet and turned over the Player hand. Natural 8. He turned over the Bank hand: natural 9.

It continued that way for a dozen hands.

I didn't win a single hand. When we stood up, I was on the rim for $70,000.

Had I been alone, I wouldn't have been at the opening session of that baccarat table.

CAROLE AND I brought our friends, Ted Koryn and Jane Stanley, to Trump's Castle. (That was before I developed such a personal distaste for The Donald that I play rarely at his casinos.)

On the afternoon of our arrival I quickly won $19,500. Great. Even then I enjoyed taking Donald Trump's money.

I cashed out and quit.

Ted Koryn, playing at my side, won $2,200. It happened in a few minutes and he was delighted.

I PERSUADED TED to follow my example by doing no more playing. He and I and our respective spouses enjoyed a gourmet dinner with fine wines. (They drink, I don't.)

We watched a show. We agreed to leave before noon the next day.

On the next morning, on the way to the checkout counter, Ted excused himself and darted into the casino. Despite his promise and my plea, he promised me he'd be in and out in five minutes.

He was almost as good as his word. Ten minutes later he walked toward me with fallen face and $650 poorer.

Hit-and-run! Hit-and-run!

You can win battles, but you're not going to win a long war. The longer you play, the larger that percentage brigade against you becomes.

IN LAS VEGAS, you'll hear the tale of the fellow who came to town, started with $80 at the dice table, built a stake of a few hundred thousand at one place, a couple of hundred thousand at another, and so forth, and today is reported to have a cool million on deposit in the Nevada National Bank.

Contrast this with the millions upon millions who have lost their bankrolls at dice tables. Sure, one in millions will make a huge killing. But on balance you want to win on every visit. You must be totally free. To move from table to table and casino to casino. And on impulse to head for the airport to take a plane—any plane to anywhere that will take you away from the action.

As I said earlier, if you're hooked on the fun and games, read no further. This book won't be of any real value to you. It is written for those few who are determined to win and who understand that they must put aside childish pleasures as part of the admission fee to the winner's circle. That's the dues.

Incidentally, Charley Kandel died a few years ago. His funeral service took place in New York City, and the large room at Riverside Memorial Chapel was packed with casino owners, managers and players—many of whom had flown cross-country for the ten-minute ritual.

He's dead but the wisdom of his words lives on:

IF YOU WANT TO GET RICH,
GET RICH IN THE DARK*

To which I add:
—AND DO IT ALONE.

---

*My old (Manhattan's) New School for Social Research classmate, Mario Puzo, read the original manuscript of this book. He liked this phrase so much he used it a dozen times in his next novel.

32

THE WINNER'S INSTINCT

I'm a believer in what I call my energy level. This is different from my fatigue level—a subtle difference to be sure, but a difference.

When my energy level is low, I know deep in my heart-of-hearts that I shouldn't gamble. When my energy is low, resistance is low and discipline tends to erode.

Cards going against you? Stick around; they'll change. Dice choppy? Eventually it has to be different! *Applesauce!*

This is the time to run. To your room. Or to a movie. Or to shop. Or to the airport.

But get out of the casino.

The same is true when you're tired. Now, you can be tired from lack of sleep or from the emotional wear and tear of gambling. But the energy level? Think of yourself as a human battery. You're charged up when you arrive. You concentrate and think and feel and maneuver and suffer and triumph. You're using that mental electricity all the time. When it has been dissipated, it's time to return home and give yourself time to recharge.

AS A CASINO PLAYER, you are always bucking a minus computation. Even the most favorable game is really just the least unfavorable.

In the golden days of Damon Runyon there was a fellow named Nicholas Andrea Dandolos. He was better known as Nick the Greek.

In sixty years, it is said that he won and lost nearly four hundred million dollars.

I used to watch him gamble. He was a "Don't" player at the dice tables. He listened to the stickman call the outcome but he rarely glanced at the dice. Instead, he stared into the distance across the room with a bored expression on his face.

Don't players die just as broke as *Do* players.*

Nick died broke.

But in his halcyon days he was bold (not reckless) and had an incredible grasp of mathematical odds on any wager.

Nick believed in good judgment and sound instincts. He is reported to have once said, "When you see a man walk into a casino with an air of quiet confidence and buy a specific amount of chips without asking whether he can cash a check later should the need arise—then proceed directly to one game and test his luck with small wagers until he's sure how it's running, keep an eye on him.

---

*An exception to the "all gamblers die broke" legend is John W. "Bet a Million" Gates. He began as a barbed-wire salesman in Texas. He never stopped gambling, winning and losing large fortunes. When he died in 1911 he was worth between $40 million and $50 million.

"He will know the game and how it's played *before* he risks his first chip. When he wins, he'll increase his stake, to take full advantage of his luck. And when he's losing, he'll bet conservatively to ride out the streak.

"Should he lose the chips he came in with, he'll quit."

Nick often remarked that no method known to humanity can change a minus expectation to a plus expectation. He knew, too, that what often separates winners from losers is attitude. Money management is a test of human character and intelligence. Winning requires the *intention* to win.

There is something primitive in the human psyche that fears success; the gods get angry if you win too much, and winning big really does scare the average person. Losers feel safer, somehow, when they're out-of-pocket. They've appeased the jealous gods, and feel virtuous because they've taken their lumps, an attitude that goes back to early childhood (mother loves you *after* you've been beaten, everyone is sorry for you when you cry, and no one hates or envies you). Winners stay cool: They have the guts to face the envy and hatred of the losers and the wrath of the gods.

Psychology was part of Nick the Greek's secret. The other part was a carefully thought-out method, a "system of plateaus"—for *keeping* some winnings. What it amounted to was this:

If he started with $500, and hit a winning cycle, he allowed his stake to build, gradually increasing his bets, until he had $1,500. Then he pocketed his original $500 and continued playing with the thousand. If he lost the thousand, he'd quit. If he ran it up still higher, $1,000 became his plateau, and the moment he lost back the thousand he quit with the remainder, no matter how much or little it was.

As to his method of increasing wagers, this was largely intuitive with Nick the Greek. Many gamblers say they don't believe in "luck." He did, and he believed, or observed, that it ran in cycles.

A comic named Lou Holtz related this experience with Nick the Greek. Lou went with Nick to a "high society" party. Downstairs, a lively orchestra played the popular hit songs of the day so that some of the season's most widely known debutantes could dance. Upstairs in the master bedroom, a high-stakes dice game took place on the bed.

With sinking feelings, Lou Holtz watched Nick lose just under $250,000. (Translate that into maybe two million of today's dollars!) The game ended and the players straggled downstairs.

"I sat on the bed in a state of shock," Lou Holtz reported. "Poor Nick. My good friend had just lost a quarter of a million dollars. I was sick. I felt awful.

"Finally I dragged myself downstairs. When I raised my head to look, there was Nick laughing and dancing with a woman nearly a foot taller than he was. He was bouncing around the dance floor with more vigor than any of the other dancers.

"I couldn't believe my eyes. I shouldered my way through the dancers and grabbed his arm. "For God's sake, Nick! How can you dance? You just lost a fortune!'

"Nick looked at me with genuine surprise, and then with a twinkle of amusement in his eyes. he said, 'Lou, your life doesn't go with it!'"

Nick the Greek also used to say, "The only difference between a winner and a loser is—character."

In this book we call it self-discipline.

WHY DO YOU GAMBLE?

The serious gambler is a man who is at war with Chance and all her bitchy whimsy.... In the casino there is, whether he wins or loses, certainty; he consults the table, which speaks to him through the dice, as the Greeks consulted oracles, and the oracle rewards him by telling him now, not next week or next year, whether the choices he is making are right or wrong.

—William Pearson in his gambling novel,
The Muses of Ruin

33

"DON'T" DICE PLAYERS

My very sharp friend, Nick Darvas, wrote a book titled *Wall Street: The Other Las Vegas*. Its thesis is that, like the casino, the stockbroker makes money on each and every transaction. Whether you buy stocks or sell them; whether you gain profits or suffer losses, the broker collects his commission.

At the height of the 1929-1934 Depression, comedian Eddie Cantor wrote a funny book about the stock market catastrophe with the title *Where Are The Customers' Yachts?* His point was that the brokers were still living in high style but their customers weren't faring nearly as well.

Despite the general calamity, there were sharp traders who made millions in the crash. They were the "short" sellers like Floyd Odlum.

When you buy a stock in the stock market, you're a "long" buyer. You buy it with the hope and/or belief that it will rise in price so you can one day sell it at a profit: the difference between what you paid for it and what you receive for it. I liken you to the "do" or "pass line" bettor at craps. You're betting that the shooter will make points...will be a winner.

To "short" a stock means that you sell it without owning it, hoping it will go down in price so you can then buy it and deliver it.

I liken "short" sellers to "Don't" players at the dice tables. They're betting the shooter will be a loser.

"Short" sellers and "Don't" players are not terribly popular.

However, while a large short sale of a stock can affect its price, a series of "Don't pass" and "Don't come" wagers have no effect whatever on the outcome of the toss of the dice.

Still, you'll always find the "Don't" player acting like an outsider. Everyone is cheering for the shooter to make his point while the "Don't" man is hoping he never makes it.

The reality is that it is often prudent to go "Don't." But many will *never* bet that way.

As you know, the odds against "pass line" and "Don't pass" wager is approximately the same 1-1/2 percent.

In a back alley dice game, the way to bet is against the shooter. It would be the ideal way to bet at Bank Craps too, except that the casino retains its edge by barring the "12." As I mentioned earlier, this means that if a twelve is thrown on the "come out" roll, the shooter loses, but your "Don't pass" wager is a push. You don't win.

I often play "Don't" in a big way. That is, I make a "Don't pass" wager. If the shooter throws a number, I lay full odds against his making that number. I also make a "Don't come" wager. If he makes another number, the chips are moved to the rear box for that number and again I lay complete odds against the shooter repeating it.

At blackjack, you can't take the side of the house. You can't bet with the dealer against the players. But in craps, when you play "Don't" you are doing just that.

When you place the 4 or 10, the house odds are 9-to-5, giving the house a 6.67 percent edge.

When you place the 5 or 9, the house odds are 7-to-5, giving the house a 4 percent advantage.

When you place the 6 or 8, the casino lays you 7-to-6, taking only a 1.82 percent bite.

WHAT HAPPENS if you want to play the "Don't" side?

You can lay a wager against the 4 or 10 and the house will pay you 11-to-5.

Lay against the 5 or 9 and the payoff is 5-to-4. It's 6-to-5 on the 6 or 8.

When I play "Don't" I place three chips on the "Don't pass" line and then lay six more. At the same time, I bet three chips in the "Don't come" line and when the shooter throws another point, that wager is moved to a spot behind the number on the green felt table and I push six more chips to the dealer.

Again, the six chips are "free odds" money. They don't give either side an advantage.

The ideal scenario, and it happens frequently, is for the shooter to come out with a point and then throw three or four other numbers one time each and then seven out.

It's a pleasure to watch the dealer pay off each of my four or five wagers.

THERE'S ONE MORE feature that, surprisingly, few players understand. I once won a $1,000 wager with a veteran craps shooter on this one. I pointed out that if you are on the side of the shooter and have several Come bets with odds, you can take down your odds money at any time but the original Come bets are locked in. They're subject to fate: either the shooter will make the number and you'll win or he'll seven out and you'll lose.

On the "Don't" side, however, you can, at any time, take down your odds money *and the original bets.*

My friend never knew that. He'd been playing in casinos all of his adult life and he didn't know that. Mind boggling!

It's all quite understandable when you think about it. If you make a "Don't pass" wager and, for example, the shooter comes out with a four, you already have a wager in your favor, for the chances of his throwing that four before he throws a seven are one in three. So, if you're foolish enough to relieve the casino of its disadvantage, they're delighted.

If you feel nothing good is happening at the crap table and nothing good is about to happen, move to the "Don't" side. If three shooters in a row fail to make a single pass, move to "Don't" for at least one hand.

Remember too that Rule of Three. And remember that if you're wrong, you'll lose only one wager or set of wagers. On the other hand, if shooters continue to seven-out and you stay with the Pass Line crowd, you'll be ground out fast.

Try it. You may like it!

34

THE BOTTOM LINE

When I go casino-hopping, it is with the sole goal of taking home casino money. I do an unusual thing. I carry along with me a cassette recorder. After each session at the tables, I speak into it about how I'm doing and what I've done.

This is often a tremendous help to me. It gives me a hindsight I never could otherwise capture. It gives me insight into my weaknesses and strengths.

It amazes me now to listen to some of these old cassettes. In the blur that could set in after too much playing, they gave me perspective. They highlighted errors. They showed me what I was doing right. They alerted me to my repeated errors. My gaming, like all of life, is a constant educational and training process.

That's my thing. Each of us must do his own thing. It works beautifully for me, but might not work at all for you. On the other hand, when you say, "I stayed too long at the tables. I have to be more alert about leaving when I'm nicely ahead"— the very act of saying it may alert you to a more disciplined departure in the next round.

Gambling is an esoteric thing. It is a very personal experience. We each see and feel it differently.

In the excitement and when you're in action, it is sometimes necessary to clarify your objective. This should be simple: You want to leave richer than you were when you arrived.

I know chronic losers who look at me as if I'm insane when I tell them that if they depart even a single dollar ahead—they should consider it a triumph. *One dollar!* A win and thus a victory.

Casinos try to persuade you that "winning is only half the fun." Don't believe them. *Winning is everything!*

Dame Circumstance takes care of the numbers. Sometimes you'll streak lucky and come away with much more than you sought. Other times the amount will seem disappointing at first—but will seem considerably more satisfying the next day.

THIS IS WHAT happens when discipline erodes. I call it "Danger Time."

I flew to Las Vegas. I checked into the Riviera at 1 P.M. At about 10 P.M. I checked out. I was $24,860 ahead for a nine-hour visit.

Then I did that dumb thing to which I too am susceptible when I'm tired. I had a half-hour to spare. I walked to a baccarat table, stood there and called large bets. I lost. My winnings shrank.

Time had run out if I was to make my flight. I had twelve purple chips ($6,000) in my hand. The cashier's cage was only a few yards from the baccarat table, but I was too tired to care. My self-discipline had washed away. I couldn't wait to lose.

I hurried to my car.

After the plane took off, I took a count and made a final report into my cassette recorder. I was still $3,457 ahead. I knew that I could hate myself for my stupidity in losing back so much money because I so clearly violated my own rules. But I knew, too, that I would feel better the next day about winning $3,457.

I was, after all, a winner.

(I'm an ice cream freak. You can buy *two truckloads* of Ben & Jerry's ice cream cones for $3,457!)

What happens from gaming session to gaming session is important but not critical. What really counts is where you stand financially when you leave town.

35

YOUR FINAL NUMBERS

Temporary losses don't matter if you're under control. Self-discipline can overcome even those disadvantageous table odds! One of my personal rules is to try not to gamble on the last day in the casino where I have credit. And not to gamble at all in the three hours before I leave. In the incident I described in the previous chapter, time was short. Too short. And I violated my rule and paid high dues for my foolishness.

Let me tell you how my cassette recorder played an important positive role on another visit.

That trip began with a difference. During my first hour at the baccarat table, the fellow to my right held the shoe for twenty-three passes.

(In all my years of playing, I have never before or since seen or known anyone to equal that long a run.)

I was betting with him all the way—though unbelieving most of the way. Then I got lucky with dice. On to another casino and more winnings.

When I counted up I was just under $60,000 ahead. I had been in Reno less than four hours.

Jump on a plane and get out? Ah, but I was in a bind. Carole was joining me in two days. I had reserved my hotel suite for four days.

Do you see immediately how this violated my own canon of behavior? And why I say: If you're serious about winning, go alone.

I phoned my son Rory, who was playing jazz guitar in Boulder, Colorado. He agreed to fly to visit with me for a few hours the next day.

By the time he arrived, I was less than $30,000 ahead.

RORY HAS ALWAYS disapproved of my gambling. He feels that gamblers are fools—a sentiment in which I concur. He sees neither fun nor excitement in it.

It bores him.

So it was that while he was with me I didn't gamble.

He departed. Carole arrived. I won some, and I lost some. But I was locked into casino-roving and, thus, doing far too much playing. After a time, Lady Luck turned her least-pleasant face to me. I ignored my own rules. I lost. From place to place, percentages chopped away at me.

Late that night—or, rather, at 2 A.M.—we returned to the room and had begun to undress when I handed Carole a thick pack of money. "Go downstairs and go straight to the baccarat table and bet this on Player," I told her.

She did. The bet won. The uncounted money stack I gave her consisted of thirty $100 bills, so she returned to the room with $6,000.

"I just wanted to go to sleep after a winning wager," I explained.

But I was infected with the casino disease of overstimulation. I'd been in town too long. At 6 A.M. I was downstairs again and quickly lost the last of my ready cash.

Tapped out. Or, as the late great Toots Shor used to say, "Tapioca."

I returned to the suite. I sat in the living room and relayed the latest bad turn into the cassette. Then, out of curiosity, I played the whole thing back.

Early on, I had talked into it about a fellow who lost $100,000 cash at baccarat. He asked for $2,000* "get-out-of-town" money, and was given it.

But instead of getting out of town, he sat down at the table and started to play again. When he left Las Vegas, he had won back the $100,000 and another $100,000.

Chris Becker, then a supervisor at Caesars Palace told me that story observing as the moral, "A man isn't dead until his ass is cold."

A MAN ISN'T DEAD UNTIL HIS ASS IS COLD!

I thought this an amusing enough tale when I heard it to relate it to my cassette recorder. But that was when things were amusing because I was ahead nearly $60,000.

---

*This is also known as "broke money" and though you, like myself, may never avail yourself of it, you should know it exists. If you gamble a large amount of money and go broke in a casino, you can always ask for—and often get—cash enough to remove you from the scene of your disaster.

"Broke money" is not a small incidental in casino overhead. Years ago, Jack Binion reported that his Horseshoe was giving away $12,000 a month in "broke money."

Now I was out of cash and a $42,000 loser. I had come to "Divorce City" to win. I had won a goodly sum and then, like a lollipop, I had tossed my own rules into the trash basket and turned my win into a sizable and depressing loss.

A MAN ISN'T DEAD UNTIL HIS ASS IS COLD!

I thought about it. I certainly seemed "dead"—and yet I felt full of positive energy.

I knew I could tap another $20,000 worth of chips on my credit line. I did. But first I searched my own true feelings. I decided the urge to play was not the usual loser's self-destructive drive. This time, I did not intend to lose.

Downstairs I went. I had only a few hours before our scheduled departure to San Francisco.

By flight time, I had won back my $42,000, and another $7,412.

Not the sixty big ones I could have left with. But I left *a winner.*

A MAN ISN'T DEAD UNTIL HIS ASS IS COLD!

WHAT COUNTS IS THE FINAL COUNT—THE MONEY IN YOUR POCKET WHEN YOU BOARD THAT PLANE OR TAKE THAT TRAIN TO GO HOME.

36

THE FASTEST GAME
IN TOWN

Baccarat and craps. Craps and baccarat. I like em both for the money I can take from them. For a time I took most of the winnings from dice tables. Then it was mostly baccarat. Now, once again, it's craps.

Baccarat can be fast and rough, so when I just want to wet my feet I stay with dice.

"Be strong," I tell myself. "Put your blinders on and walk past the baccarat pit without making a wager."

I am a hero to myself when I do.

But then comes a time when the dice are sour and I don't have the feeling they are about to change for me. I want to recoup some dollars.

Baccarat. I would win it there. I often do.

IT'S PRONOUNCED "bac-ca-*ra*" and means zero. It is, without doubt, the fastest game in the casino. It is also the classiest, often portrayed in the movies as the continental game of glamour, sophistication and high-paced excitement.

It's a simple game. It's easier to play than its European cousin, chemin de fer.

BLACK-TIE BACCARAT, American-style, was brought to Las Vegas from Havana by a good friend of mine, the late Francis "Tommy" Renzoni.

The American version of the "big nine" game is "automatic" in that there are no decisions for the player to make with regard to the cards.

In chemin de fer, if a player's two cards total five, he or she must decide whether to ask for a third card. The draw is optional. And the player's job is to deceive the person banking the game. In American-style baccarat, the player *must* draw a card.

In chemin de fer, the gamble is limited by the amount the person holding the shoe is willing to lose. In American baccarat, you play against the casino's entire bankroll.

Moreover, the player can decide to play Bank or Player and to switch sides from hand to hand. He is thus given a chance to outguess the deck.

There is nothing mysterious about baccarat. It seems to intimidate people who haven't played it but it is a game that anyone can play. You have only two decisions to make.

1. Will you bet?
2. On which side will you bet?

You place your money on either Bank or Player and wait. Everything that happens thereafter is quite automatic, with the Caller directing, according to rules, whether or not Bank and/or Player receive a third card after the first two are dealt.

HOW MUCH CAN you bet on a hand? In some sawdust joints, the minimum is as low as $5. Others have a $20 minimum.

The maximum in some places is $10,000, and in others, $4,000.

At the Horseshoe, you can bet $25,000 a hand without making any special arrangements.

The Mirage allows a maximum of $15,000 per hand. And, of course, if you're a whale,* at some casinos you can make arrangements to bet as much as $200,000 a hand.

Baccarat is a pure guessing game. It's a heads-or-tails drama. Because of the way rules are structured, the Bank has a slight edge and will usually (but not always) win a few more hands in a shoe than the Player side.

It is startling to survey the ignorance about the game which exists even in veteran players. For example, I know a man who flies to Las Vegas once a month from Brazil.

The hotel he stays at keeps a suite for him at all times. It's called The Diplomat Suite. We'll call him Mr. Machado because that isn't his name.

At any rate, he's a big-money craps player. Even at grind hotels he plays $8,000 and $16,000 at the dice table by special arrangement.

He alternates among five casinos. At each, he has a $250,000 credit line.

He picks up his markers with cash before he leaves town.

---

*To remind you: a whale is a "big dropper" who usually has a credit line of a million dollars or more.

They love him!

He thinks he has a marvelous deal on accommodations. His primary hotel gives him extra security* protection. And his arrangement with all five hotels is that, if he is a big loser, they allow him the cost of two first class, round-trip tickets from Las Vegas to Rio de Janeiro.

If Mr. Machado is a small loser, $50,000 or less, he doesn't bother about airline tickets. If he is a large loser, he asks for and gets that cash refund. If he loses big in four casinos, he gets the cash price for two tickets from each of the four casinos!

Needless to say, over any several weeks, he loses hundreds of thousands of dollars. Needless to say, he can afford it.

In a conversation with him I mentioned that I like baccarat as much as dice. Oh, no, he explained, *they charge 5 percent on winning Bank bets at baccarat!*

If even a big-money player like Machado is *that* ignorant, it is understandable that baccarat hasn't become as popular as the other major casino table games.

It should. I happen to believe it gives you as good a shot as any game in the casino—if you're willing to win and walk.

As to the 5 percent, this is the explanation. The casino gives the Player side even odds. If you bet $100 on Player and it wins, you are paid $100.

Since the rules of the game favor the Bank side, the casino lays you 95 cents against your dollar for bets on the

---

*All things considered, security isn't bad in casinos. The MGM Grand's president, Larry Woolf, reports that his hotel and casino employs 400 security officers.

Bank side. But it would take forever to pay people 95 cents for each dollar wagered. So what they do is to pay you even money—$100 for your $100 bet—and mark up $5 against your seat (to which they give the misnomer of "commission").

(I liken this to the label "life insurance" when the fact is, no one collects until the insured person dies.)

The 5 percent isn't "commission." They pay you $1 but they should have paid you only 95 cents. The nickel they charge against you is the change you owe them. Period.

WHAT'S SO GREAT about baccarat?

For one thing, the odds against you are even smaller than those against "Do" and "Don't" pass line bets at craps.

The odds against "Player" bets are 1.35 percent and the odds against "Bank" bets are even smaller: approximately 1.20 percent.

For another thing, look at the range of the wagers you can make. In no other casino game can you put down $10,000 on either side and in less time than it takes to read this, win or lose. Win a bet on the Player's side and you're paid $10,000. Win a bet on the Bank side and you're paid $10,000 but owe $500 change. (All clear?)

In no other game can you bet comparatively small amounts—guess wrong and lose ten bets in a row—and then have a maximum high enough to allow you to make one big bet and win back all your losses, and then some.

It's quick and it's clean.

Results often run in streaks. This can break the novice. He observes that the Bank has won four or five times and is convinced that it's time for Player to win. But Bank can win another four or five times. Or the pattern might run Bank, Player, Bank, Player, Bank, Bank, Player, Player. (Veteran players call this "chopping.")

To win at baccarat certainly requires luck and perhaps a certain unconscious sense of the rhythm of the cards. People who believe they have systems or try to count against a shoe containing eight decks of cards are destined to be losers.

The action and suspense are the greatest.

Baccarat has style. Note the atmosphere with the dealers in formal attire. It is the casino's "class game." It has status.

It can also make or lose big fortunes for the casino.

SOME YEARS AGO, a Las Vegas casino on the Strip had a happy experience. Twelve men and women flew to town from Japan. They occupied all the player seats. They spoke Japanese and they talked to each other with vigor and animation.

At the time, that casino's limit was $4,000. But now twelve players each bet $4,000 so that they were, in fact, betting $48,000 per hand.

They had a system. Obviously someone had worked out a strategy to destroy the casino. They did all kinds of figuring with felt-tipped pens on rectangular-shaped pads, and the chatter never ceased. When they quit fourteen hours after they'd begun, the English-speaking croupiers hadn't understood one word that had been spoken. The supervisors understood only one thing: the group had lost $1,250,000, almost to the penny.

The casino quickly sought and hired a Japanese-speaking dealer. They needn't have bothered. That particular group has never returned. The Japanese dealer was retained because one of the executives pointed out that two million Japanese visit Las Vegas each year.

ASIANS LOVE BACCARAT. It has become the favorite game of their largest gamblers. I recall one group who flew each month from Hong Kong to the Desert Inn. The hotel reserved two entire floors for the group. Wives and girl-friends were restricted to one floor—the men occupied the other.

When the group sat down to play, all showed respect for the leader. He made the decision as to which side to bet on. The others would all bet on that side. It would have been an insult to him for anyone to do otherwise!

When it was all over, several million dollars changed hands. And, by prior arrangement, 20 percent of their loss was refunded to the group.

Was this group important to the D.I.? I'll tell you how important. Red is a lucky color to the Chinese. So the Desert Inn changed the felt on their baccarat table to red, and bought red chairs which sat on red carpeting!

AT CAESARS PALACE, I used to watch a man from Indonesia bet $30,000 a hand. Over a period of years, I personally watched him lose more millions than I have fin-gers and toes.

One evening he said, "Give me two hundred more."

The dealer pushed two hundred yellow ($1,000) chips toward him and leaned over to report, "That makes one million, Mr. D."

"I know, I know," he said impatiently.

He lost the $200,000 in less than fifteen minutes.

It was nearly midnight and I retired to my room for some shut-eye. At about 5 A.M. I awoke, shaved, showered, and returned to the baccarat pit.

In my absence, Mr. D. had lost another million.

What fascinated me about Mr. D. is that he himself owns casinos on the island of Macao.

Why then would he gamble away millions of dollars in a game whose odds he should understand better than most players?

I was puzzled.

Someone who knew him well gave me this explanation: "All his life he has conquered everything he confronted. He just can't believe he can't beat this game!"

BACCARAT HAS GROWN in popularity. At one Atlantic City casino I have seen as many as five full tables in action, with people waiting in line for seats. For a while, visitors from Latin America dominated the tables but now it's obviously the favorite game for Asians. Many casinos have offices in Hong Kong and often fly full junket planes from that city. They look for some action at the Pai Gow* tables but they know the big money will be wagered at baccarat.

Then there is Pai Gow Poker of which a unique feature is that the role of banker rotates counterclockwise among the players and house dealer after each game. In other words, each player has a chance to bank a bet against all other players, including the house dealer.

---

*Pai Gow is an ancient Chinese game. Literally translated, Pai Gow means "dominoes nine." It's the forerunner of the game we know as dominoes. It also contains some of the elements of baccarat.

Pai Gow is exciting enough, but unfamiliarity with its seemingly complicated rules seems to have restricted the action mostly to visitors from the Orient.

POSTSCRIPT: The following news is for mini-baccarat aficionados. It seems that Bally's Las Vegas has introduced a new Quick-Draw mini-baccarat game. According to Huey Mahl, writing in *Gaming Today*, the game eliminates the 5 percent "commission" collected on winning Bank wagers. The drawing rules are simplified. It doesn't matter what third card is dealt to Player. Both sides draw if they have five or less. The odds against Player and Bank are equal. They've been reduced to 1.16 percent.

The game was created by Richard Lofink and his computer-expert son Kurt. I asked Lofink where the casino got its vigorish and he explained that instead of the 5 percent commission on winning Bank wagers, there is a Bally's "bar" hand similar to the "bar 12" rule on the "Don't" side in craps. This is a "bar 2" when either Bank of Player wins with a total of 2 (2-1 or 2-0). The house wins these hands.

A 2-2 tie hand is a push but a winner in the tie box.

There is a proposition bet box where you can bet on the advent of a "bar 2" hand occurring for either side. A 2-1 or 2-0 pays 40-to-1. It loses on a 2-2 tie

The "natural" bet has been restored. You can once again wager on either a Player natural (8 or 9)or a Bank natural (8 or 9. This pays 4-to-1, but only if the natural is a winner. Thus if you bet on Player's natural and Player turns up an 8 which is beaten by the Bank hand of 9, you lose your bet. A natural tie (8 vs. 8 or 9 vs. 9) will also lose. On the other hand, if you bet say on a Player natural and the

Player draws a natural 9 over Bank's natural 8, your payoff is a healthy 12-to-1.

Cards are bar-coded and they're read by a scanner on the bottom lip of the shoe as they're dealt. A signal is sent to a small computer and the numbers displayed instantly on a large TV monitor for all to see. The computer rather than the dealer announces the winning side.

As with all new games, it will take a while to see if this one catches on.

Above: A sample of the bar-coded baccarat card that will be read by a scanner.

37

ON TIPPING AND EMPLOYEE MORALE

All of my adult life, I've had a certain contempt for money. Sure, I've been uncomfortable without it, for it does provide pleasure and comfort. But money itself has never been my primary concern: neither accumulating it nor accumulating the things it buys. I'm not a collector and there are few material possessions that I couldn't do without. (A few years ago I sold a book publishing business for twelve million dollars, and quickly spent, gave away or gambled away on the stock market's junk bonds at least half of it.)

All of this by way of explaining that my attitudes need not be your attitudes on tips and tipping.

There is no reason to tip dealers and no need to tip dealers.

That being said, let me add that I'm one of the most generous tippers I know. I tip early and sometimes I tip often. I do it by making two-way hard-way bets for the dealers at the dice table and $100 dealer bets at baccarat.

If a stickman or croupier tries to hustle me with the not-so-often-heard anymore, "Why not make a little bet for the boys?" there is no way I tip.

My tipping is instinctive and voluntary, and I resent anyone pressuring me to tip.

Tipping can't change the face of a single card or the turn of a single die. It cuts into your winnings.

Why do it then? You needn't.

Why do I do it? Because usually I like dealers and starters and I enjoy having them share my good fortune when I have been lucky. I want to feel a positive atmosphere at the tables. I enjoy them rooting for me.

I'm known widely enough so that when I lose, the dealers know they're losing too.

My tips have come to as much as $4,000 on a winning trip.

TIPPING WAS ONCE permitted in British casinos, but now it's prohibited. The British theory is that tipping dealers gives them a vested interest in the outcome of the play and might lead to collusion between dealers and players.

Nobody has offered any collusion to me but it isn't a bad feeling to know that several dealers at a table genuinely want me to win.

I would doubt that the British ban on tipping helped dealer morale.

Employee morale is important to the player. You don't want a listless, inattentive crew who are angry with their bosses and bored with your action. It will tend to communicate itself to the way you play.

Years ago, management ruled casino personnel through fear and intimidation. Dealers could be dismissed on the slightest pretext or on no pretext at all. If there was the slightest back talk, a supervisor would say, "There are ten people waiting for your job!"

Some casinos complained that turnover of employees was scaling 100 percent annually. The firings were described as "non-voluntary" turnover. Those who endured public scolding and management nastiness stayed only for the money. There was little other job satisfaction.

That was when Las Vegas had salary levels for school teachers that were said to be the highest in the land. Despite this, teachers were deserting classrooms by the score to take higher-paying casino dealer jobs.

Today casinos are starved for good personnel. There aren't enough experienced people to fill the available jobs.

Recently I took my entire office staff to Foxwoods Mashantucket Pequot reservation near Ledyard, Connecticut. Its now the largest casino in America and the second largest in the world. (The largest is the Genting Highlands in Malaysia.) Foxwoods' two casinos stretch further than you'd want to walk. More than 2.5 acres of its 7.6 acres are given over to slot machines. At this writing these number 3,879 and there are many more on the way.

I was betting $5,000 a hand at Blackjack with dealers who, a few months ago, didn't know a deck contained 52 cards. Our host had never been in a casino in his life before he got his first job there as a security guard.

The craps personnel seemed to have their minds on everything but the games they were dealing. When I handed a dealer a yellow chip ($1,000) to place $300 wagers on three numbers, the lady dealer erroneously returned my $100 change twice.

Personnel were so relaxed that it seems everyone was talking to a fellow-employee. Whether at the tables, the slots or the cashier cage, I found myself waiting for attention while employees chatted with each other.

And yet this huge operation, operating with very few truly experienced staffers, is earning profits of more than one million dollars a day.

RECENTLY AT A gaming conference, an expert in employee relations described an experience one of her colleagues encountered.

He was assigned to study conditions at a lumber factory. When he arrived there, an ambulance was at the entrance and someone was being carried out on a stretcher.

"What happened?" he asked.

He was told the worker had talked back to a supervisor "and the supervisor decked him."

The expert expected to find very low morale inside the plant. Instead he encountered a very happy crew.

It took time for him to understand what was happening. What was happening was that the entire three shifts were getting even with their supervisors.

There was a machine in the plant called "the hog." Bad timber was supposed to be fed into the hog, where it was quickly chopped into sawdust.

The crews held contests to see who could slip the most of the very best logs into the hog. This was done, of course, when the supervisors weren't looking.

"Feeding the hog" is something I came upon, though rarely, in casinos where personnel were resentful of their executives. They would make little gestures, turn over unrequested cards at Blackjack when they knew you needed more than you showed if you were to beat them, and so forth.

I was never comfortable in that situation. Fortunately for all concerned, casino management today has a renewed understanding that morale must be high if the crew is to work as an effective team.

ALLOW ME A moment of nostalgia. I am reminded of a time, many years ago, when Tommy Renzoni was about to close the Sands' baccarat game for the night. Baccarat wasn't a twenty-four-hour proposition in those days—and even today the game isn't opened in some casinos until noon or 1 P.M.

I had done well. "How about one more shoe, Tommy?"

Tommy turned to his crew. "Do you want to deal one more shoe for Lyle?"

The dealers were exhausted. They looked at each other and nodded "yes" and they were gracious about it.

A dealer named Patrick was having difficulty keeping his eyes open. He went on his relief break and I was doing well with the shoe when suddenly I announced: "A thousand-dollar bet for the dealers on Player."

I held the shoe. After a stunned silence, someone said, "You mean on Bank?"

"No. I mean on Player."

I dealt Player a total of 2. I dealt Bank a total of 1. The third card for each of them was a 9.

Player had a final total of 1, beating Bank, which had broken to 0.

It was at this moment that Patrick returned to the table, still looking as though he needed toothpicks to keep his eyelids up. One of the dealers beckoned to him and whispered in his ear: "Stuart just made a thousand-dollar bet for us and it won!"

Patrick woke up like a shot. The smile on his face was almost worth the $2,000.

Today, he's a dealer at another casino. When I first played there some years later, no more than a few minutes passed when he said, "Do you remember that night—"

"I was just thinking about it," I said.

Patrick broke into another broad grin.

It's a pleasant memory.

38

WHERE THERE'S SMOKE
THERE'S A LOSER

Anybody remember the song, "Cigarettes, Whuskey and Wild Wild Women"?

I don't smoke. I happen to believe cigarette smokers are natural-born losers. If you're a cigarette smoker, you may disagree. Incidentally, the percentage of deaths attributed to cigarette smoking is higher in Las Vegas than in any other city in America.

Fortunately, smart casino owners have responded to player demands and some casinos boast about their large nonsmoking slot areas and their nonsmoking blackjack and crap tables. You still leave casinos smelling of smoke but the odor isn't quite as strong.

You don't agree that folks who are destroying themselves with smokes will also tend to destroy themselves at gaming?

Watch me as I often profit by betting opposite them. I'll make money while you disagree.

DON'T DISAGREE with me about alcohol. It's free and plentiful in every casino. And it's for all the players at all the tables, except you.

You want to have a clear mind.

Contrary to the soft soap about a drink or two "clearing your head" or "relaxing you," there is no way that alcohol* will do anything for you except dull your reflexes, your intuition, your true feelings, and your discipline.

Drinking while gambling will not only help you to lose but it will make the loss seem less painful.

Drink all the booze you want to drink. At home. At the office. At your local pub.

Do not drink while you gamble.

End of sermon.

THOSE "WILD WILD women" in that song?

Welcome to them.

---

*The Commission on the Review of the National Policy Toward Gambling found a relationship between gambling and alcohol consumption. "People who bet," said the report, "say they consume alcohol on four times as many days as people who don't bet at all. As the dollar volume of betting increases, so does alcohol consumption. It is impossible to state whether gambling activities increase alcohol consumption or vice versa but the relationship is strong."

39

MORE ABOUT BACCARAT

When I play baccarat, I like to limit myself to two complete shoes. I don't care to enter a game in the middle of a shoe. I like to keep score.

Years ago in Europe, and particularly at the spielbank casinos of Bad Homburg and Wiesbaden (the latter is the only major casino that ever tried to cheat me!), I used to look with some disdain at those people at roulette tables who compulsively kept records of every turn of the wheel. (Old-time faro players kept scorecards with buttons, but that suicidal game is almost obsolete today.)

Today, I rarely play baccarat without keeping score.

The scorecard (called *Table de Banque* by dealers who can't speak any other word of French) talks to me. It tells me things I need to know. It alerts me to trends and possibilities.

Play two full shoes and then take a walk. Only if you are iron-disciplined about yourself and have won a lot of money and have carefully segregated a small amount which if you lose you'll walk—should you remain.

OVER AND OVER and over again I have watched winners turned into losers because they stayed too long.

Okay, you're sitting down. You've begun to play the guessing game. I will now share with you the complete results (except for ties) of 160 shoes that I've played at various times.

Total hands dealt on which there were decisions (in other words, ignoring ties) were 11,475.

5,754 hands were won by the Bank side.

5,721 hands were won by the Player side.

If you bet $100 on each hand and won every Bank hand, you'd have been paid a net of $546,630. If you had won every Player hand you'd have been paid $572,100.

In this case, there were an unusually large number of shoes that were aberrations. That is, where the Player won far more hands than are called for by probability statistics.

Facing are the sequences in the 160 full shoes that I played.

For one thing, if you look at column three you'll see that a 2-time sequence will occur a little less than half as many times as a one-time sequence. A 3-timer half as many as a two. A 4-timer half as many as a three. A 5-time sequence half as many times as a four.

"So what?" you say. "That's after the fact. How can this help me?"

Let me tell you how it has occasionally helped me.

I've been halfway through a shoe and not doing particularly well. I knew that I needed to chance some larger bets and to win most of them if I was to leave the table a winner. The scorecard talked to me. It confirmed to me that the shoe was chopping like crazy. But I noticed that single Banks had come up eleven times and a double Bank had come up only twice.

SEQUENCES:	BANK	TOTAL BANK PLAYER	TOTAL	HANDS*
1 time	1,506	1,532	3,038	3,038
2 times	699	712	1,411	2,822
3 times	348	376	724	2,172
4 times	179	152	331	1,324
5 times	94	80	174	870
6 times	48	48	96	576
7 times	29	23	52	364
8 times	7	9	16	128
9 times	3	5	8	72
10 times	2	2	4	40
11 times	1	2	3	33
15 times	1	1	2	30
	2,917	2,942	5,859	11,469

Now, in all of my tedious card analysis, I didn't recall a single full shoe scorecard in which Bank didn't average almost half as many 2s as 1s. Remembering that the improbable does happen, I knew it was possible. But my experience went against it.

So what did I do?

I sat out hands until Bank won. Then I placed a large bet on Bank. I was looking for that sequence of two Banks in a row.

---

*Ties also came up a total of 868 times.

I made this bet four times and won three. At $2,000 a crack I was $4,000 ahead for my scorecard-reading. More, since I believed the Bank was due for sequences of 2 (and no more), immediately after being paid for that second-in-a-row Bank win, I made a smaller bet on Player. Again I won three out of four.

It pays to know what's happening. In this case, acting on my observation paid me a profit of $4,600 after so-called commissions on the $4,000.

Ignorance can be costly.

HERE ARE SOME observations I can make after many years of playing the game.

1. "Starters" or shills are nice people. They don't affect your chances either way. They're used in Nevada but are not allowed in Atlantic City. One effect of this is that in A.C., if you sit at a baccarat table to start a game going, you must hold the shoe through all of its deals—or until another player sits down and you deal a Player hand.

2. Once the cards are shuffled, laced, cut and deposited into the shoe, *the die is cast* (to use my favorite old cliché from "Bomba the Jungle Boy"). What happens thereafter depends on which side you bet and how much you bet.

3. If you are guessing wrong, sit it out for a while. Sit, watch and don't bet.

4. If you start with a certain stake and you've lost a part of it and don't feel good at all about the game, you are under no contract to remain. Leave at any time.

That's one thing in your favor about casinos. They're always there for you to take a shot at their money but they can't take a shot at yours except when you decide to allow them to.

40

THE "IF ONLY" SYNDROME

Many years ago, Victor Lownes flew to New York from London. I met him at Kennedy Airport and we drove for nearly three hours to my wife Carole's beautiful but isolated weekend house in Stuyvesant, New York, where I'm currently writing this book.

There, cut off from phone calls, mail and visitors, we worked together without interruption for four days. Our purpose was to revise a book written by Victor that already had been published in England.

The British publisher titled it *Playboy Extraordinary*. We called it *The Day the Bunny Died*.

In its pages, Victor described the near collapse of the Playboy empire when it lost its license to operate casinos in London. The story is a fascinating tale of bumbling executives and bumbling flunkies. Hugh Hefner has always surrounded himself with them.

During the time we were together, Victor and I had time to discuss casino gaming in depth. The London casino he opened and directed was, in its time, the most profitable casino in the world. It threw off a profit of something in excess of 30 million dollars a year.

Victor doesn't gamble. Even when he plays backgammon (he beats me regularly!) he won't play with anyone his equal, for that would pose the threat of a loss. When they were still friends, he even stopped playing with Hugh Hefner when the latter's game improved.

Small wonder that the *Guinness Book of World Records* listed Victor Lownes as the highest-paid business executive in England!

After Lownes was unceremoniously fired, Hugh Hefner telephoned him from California at 4 A.M. London time to explain why the firing was necessary. Playboy would sacrifice Victor to save the casino license. (They lost both Victor *and* the license.)

At the time of his dismissal, Victor managed to stash aside coffee-and-cake money. He'd accumulated a tidy nest egg exceeding five million dollars.

What does Victor Lownes think of gambling?

"Expensive entertainment," he says with finality.

Diversion. Amusement. Costly thrills.

But can't the customer ever win?

"There's no way to beat the house out of its inexorable percentages," he will tell you.

"How about the people who actually walk out of the casino winners?"

"Our best customers!" he declared. "Those can be considered as having taken out casino loans. We know the winners will return because they believe they have discovered the secret of defeating the casino. They're hooked! In the long run, only the casino wins."

A CASINO EXECUTIVE named Richard Favero wouldn't disagree. Favero's attitude is "Make sure the customers are happy," he tells his staff. "Never mind that they are winners. That's a temporary aberration."

There was the time a player had lost a lot of money playing baccarat. He asked for a new shoe midway in the dealing. Favero agreed.

The player had enough chips for one very large wager. He made it and won.

Favero was undisturbed. "Let him enjoy it," he said, really meaning it. "He'll be back."

A young Japanese player named Mizumo arrived one day with a $200,000 bankroll. He lost $190,000 of it at baccarat. Then his fortune changed. He won back the $190,000 and $600,000 more.

Some less experienced managers might have gotten into a deep funk. They might have muttered incantations against all the dealers involved.

Dick Favero told his supervisors: "He's got the monkey on his back. Every winner has. Wait. Someday he'll come back to us and give us back our money. Just be sure that, for now, he is well treated and gets everything he wants."

Pearl Harbor for Mr. Mizumo came sooner than anyone had anticipated. Three weeks later he phoned from Hawaii to announce that he was returning.

"Get my suite ready for me!" he said, cheerfully. "I'm coming back this time to win the whole damned casino!"

"How much are you bringing?" one of the hosts couldn't resist asking.

"Just enough! The same lucky two hundred grand I came with last time," Mizumo said.

A special suite was made ready. A Japanese cook was employed to prepare Japanese food for him.

Mizumo arrived with a broad smile on his face. For several sessions he won and lost modest amounts. Then the slippage began. He lost the $200,000 and wired Tokyo for more money.

Within three weeks he lost back $582,000 of the $600,000 he'd won.

It was the same old story, but it was new to him.

41

I BLOW TWO TOURNAMENTS

Let me once more remind you about my "Rule of Three."

If either Player or Bank side wins three hands in a row, your proper move is either to bet on and hope for a fourth in that sequence or not to bet at all.

Do I always follow my own rules? Hell, no. Several years ago the Sands in Atlantic City held a World Championship of Gaming.

It was an exciting tournament. You entered the contest for one game. If you came in first, you won a $15,000 prize and a chance to compete against the tournament winners of craps, blackjack and roulette. The winner of that four-way contest would receive another $25,000 prize.

I entered the baccarat division. It required a $2,000 buy-in.

Fifty-six people entered, so each table had 14 players.

I was the big winner at my table, so I went into the final round with three competitors. The rules called for 80 hands to be dealt.

One finalist tapped out at hand 70. A second tapped out after hand 75. Only two of us remained and I was far ahead in chips.

Twice during the game, the shoe had come to me after the Player side won three consecutive times. I bet Player. Each time I won my bet and lost the shoe.

Only two hands to go. The shoe came to me. Player had come up four times.

I glanced up at the spectators. There were at least one hundred. They were quiet in anticipation. An oil painting.

I could make a modest bet on Player. Or, at worst, a tiny bet on Bank. I pretty much had the tournament locked up.

So what did I do? I looked at those hundred faces staring at me and my ego got to me. Suddenly I was James Bond! I bet $2,850 on Bank—and promptly dealt a natural 8 to Player.

The shoe moved. The last hand was also Player but by this time I was in shock! I had clearly thrown away the First Prize for no rational reason. I would characterize it as "gambling behavior." It's irrational. It's crazy.

Don't do as I *do*: do as I *say*!

AN AMUSING AFTERMATH. Several months later I broke my left leg. I was on the island of Jamaica where, exactly ten years earlier almost to the minute and the hour, I had fallen on the street in Port Maria and broke my left leg for the first time!

The same local doctor came to give me a shot of pain killer. The same local people helped me into the ambulance. I was driven over the Junction Road to a hospital in

Kingston where the same surgeon and the same anesthetist performed the operation to pin the leg.

My son, Rory, flew down to be at my side. (Daughter Sandra Lee had been at my side when I came out of the first operation.)

I was under heavy anesthesia and mumbling nothing but gibberish. Then, Rory tells me, I suddenly announced in a loud, clear voice, "Only two more hands and I would have won the tournament!"

THAT WORLD CHAMPIONSHIP of Gambling was held at the Sands of Atlantic City. You entered one of four games (baccarat, blackjack, craps, or roulette) and the person winning the most money in each game would play all games against the other three. The Championship was won by Xen Angelidis, a man from my town of Fort Lee, New Jersey. We live in the same community and have since become friends.

There was a time I didn't enter tournaments because I couldn't compete with the teams of six or eight who would be there every time. These days, most casino managers are more sophisticated. Frequently the tournaments are by invitation only and don't require an entry fee. By making them "invitational," those teams who, too often, would manage to grab the top prizes are eliminated.

At baccarat, for example, two cohorts would sit at the same table and one would make the minimum bet on Bank and one the minimum bet on Player. On the last hand, each would bet all their remaining chips, one on Bank and one on Player. As often as not, one would be #1 at the table and move on to the next level where, often, another member of the team would have advanced to this table and the pair would repeat the simple strategy.

At dice, one would play minimum bets on the line and the other the same bet on the Don't pass line.

It worked because in those days, and very often, even today, if you double your buy-in, your chances of winning the big cake are excellent.

Tournament players are smarter these days.

XEN ANGELIDIS AND I have been in several tournaments together. Let me tell you about the most recent, held on September 17, 1994.

By now you know that I don't care much for Donald Trump. After some personal experiences with him, I call him Pinnochio.

Nevertheless the recent $500,000 Baccarat Invitational at the Taj Mahal was too tempting to resist. The entry fee was $5,000 and the buy-in for each of three rounds was $1,000. And, of course, you kept anything you won.

First prize was $325,000. Second prize was $100,000. All those who survived to the final round would receive something ranging from a third prize of $20,000 to seventh to twelfth prizes of $5,000.

Apart from the size of the prizes, what I liked was that it would all take place in one day. No stretching to keep you chained to the casino. (There isn't much else to do in Atlantic City except watch TV, walk the boardwalk, or stare at seagulls from ocean-front suites. There isn't one movie theater in the entire city!)

The first round took place at noon. There were one hundred entrants.(So the casino collected its half-million dollars worth of prizes in full from the entry fees.)

Five from each of four tables would advance to the semi-finals. In addition, losers could pay $2,000 for a re-entry first round.

I won the first round with the largest win at my table, $1,840. I had come close to doubling the $1,000 entry fee. Here is my first round card.

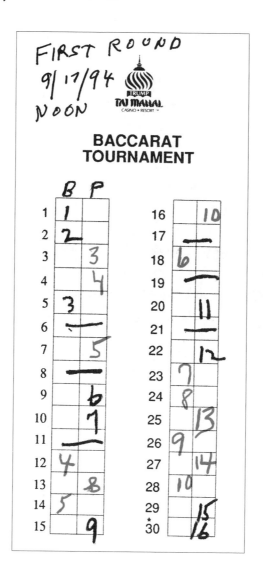

The tournament consisted of only 30 hands for each round.

Patience is the name of the game in this one. I made minimum ($25) wagers and occasionally a $50 wager until twelve or fourteen hands have been played. Then I bet larger amounts.

My card is reproduced on page 262. Note that I won only five of the first 15 hands—but eleven of the next 14.

I made a large bet on hand 28 that lost. I made one half that size on hand 29. I won. I was in third place—just where I needed to be to qualify for the so-called "Championship Round."

After 29-hands, the game is halted, bank commissions are collected, and a supervisor counts and calls out the amount held by each player. (By now, several had tapped out and left the table.)

Wagers on the last (30th) hand are made "in secret." That is, they're written on a small slip of paper so no other player knows what anyone has wagered until all the slips are in, and then the amounts are announced by the supervisor.

I had $1,383 after the 29th hand. A lady on the far side of the table had $1,119. By now, only five of us remained. The fifth player had $621 so he was out of it. The reason being that the maximum wager on Player or Bank was $500 and on tie it was $50—so that a win of $500 or a tie that paid the maximum of $200 wouldn't be enough to make Mr. Fifth Place a contender.

Ms. Four, however, was a major threat to me. I had to wager enough so that no matter what she won, I'd be ahead of her.

It was the last hand of this round. It wasn't the last hand of the shoe.

I covered myself with a $40 tie wager. Everything in me wanted to bet "Player" but Bank had won four in a row. I hoped she would bet on Bank. I bet $300.

If she bet the maximum allowed of $500 on the Bank side, and the Bank won, I'd have $1,643 and she'd have $1,619.

That's the way I figured it and that's the way I bet.

I turned to Jon Gilbert and Carole who stood behind the rope.

"I don't like this," I said. "I want very strongly to bet Player but I've got to respect my own "Rule of Three.""

She was the last person at the table to turn in her secret bet. Knowing that she'd have no chance to outwager me if Bank won, she finally also bet $40 on tie and $200 on Player.

Player won.

She ended up in third place with $1,381. I ended up in fourth place with $1,043.

Unlike the tournament described earlier in this chapter, I had "done the right thing" according to my "Rule of Three" principle. I didn't feel nearly as bad losing this as I had felt losing the other.

Here is the card reflecting the semi-final I lost. Note that I won 17 hands and lost 13. There was only one tie. I should have easily won first or second place this round but my wagers were too conservative.

SEMI-FINALS
9/17/'94
730PM

TRUMP TAJ MAHAL CASINO • RESORT ™

BACCARAT TOURNAMENT

	BANK	PLAYER		BANK	PLAYER
1	1		16		8
2		1	17		9
3		2	18		10
4		3	19		11
5		4	20		12
6	2		21	9	
7	3	5	22		13
8		6	23		14
9	4		24	16	
10	5		25		15
11	6		26	11	
12		7	27	12	
13	7		28	13	
14	8		29	14	
15	/		30		16

The final round started at midnight.

Carole and I stood behind the rope, rooting for Xen Angelidis, who had made it.

One would assume that this dozen would be more sophisticated than the earlier groups and most of them were. But a man with a mustache and a big, awful-smelling cigar, made some early maximum wagers. Within ten hands he'd built his $1,000 into $3,600.

"He has it made," I said to Carole. "If he only has the good sense to hold on to what he has, he has it made. He's won the $325,000!"

Sure enough, Mr. Cigar started wisely making $25 wagers. Now, all he had to do was watch the piles of chips in front of the other players. If anyone got close to him, he could match their wagers to the extent that they bet first. That way, they could never catch up.

It was in the bag. Or was it?

A man standing next to me said, "I know him. He'll blow it. He plays too aggressively."

Sure enough, a few hands later he was wagering $500 a hand again. He lost. And again. He lost.

By the last hand, a man on his right had accumulated about $2,600. A strikingly beautiful Asian woman on his left was a close second. (She had never stopped waving her scorecard in the air to waft away his cigar smoke but she hadn't spoken a word of complaint.)

The man won $325,000. The lady won $100,000. Mr. Cigar, who should have taken First Prize, managed only to win $20,000.

I CALL THIS "tournament behavior." I've observed it again and again.

I recall vividly the final round of a craps tournament. A preppie-looking fellow—the only player at the table wearing a necktie—spurted ahead. The buy-in was $5,000 and soon he had more than $50,000 in chips in front of him.

"He has it made," I whispered to Carole. "If only he has sense enough to conserve what he's won."

He didn't. He continued to make maximum wagers with or against the shooters and to take (or lay) maximum odds.

Five minutes before the one-hour tournament was to end, a warning bell was sounded. It was too late to warn him of anything. He'd tapped out and left the table.

He had just thrown away a $100,000 first prize.

THE TAJ MAHAL has nine baccarat tournaments scheduled for the next twelve months. Other Atlantic City casinos are doing similar things.

Most of these are invitational, no-entry fee, no buy-in tournaments. Some are $100,000 "winner take all" contests. Others offer $125,000 or $150,000 broken down into three or five or eight prizes.

Baccarat tournaments are exciting. They're fun. And the price of the no-entry, no buy-in ones is certainly right!

Someday a casino will announce a tournament with a $1,000,000 First Prize. They'll look for 100 players willing to pay $10,000 entry fees.

I'll be there!

42

I WIN A TOURNAMENT

On March 12, 1994, Carole and I were on the junket to Scottsdale, Arizona that I described earlier in these pages. We cut the pleasurable journey short so I could return to Atlantic City for Bally's first Invitational Grand VIP Baccarat Tournament .

I was on a streak. Could I miss competing in this one? I couldn't.

Each round consisted of thirty hands rather than a full shoe. My first round, with a $1,000 buy-in, was played at 2 P.M. I was one of the top five of the fourteen at our table at the end of 30 hands, so I qualified for the semifinal round.

This was played at 8 o' clock. Here, six of the fourteen would go on to the finals. I came in 4th.

The final round was dramatic. It began with a $3,000 buy-in. Twelve players competed, and they had come from all over the world: Mexico, Hong Kong, and Caracas were among the places represented.

Early on, as others moved ahead, I made a daring wager with half of my stake. I lost. I made another large wager, and lost again. An observer watching the table might well assume I was finished.

Flashback to a baccarat tournament years before at the Tropicana in Las Vegas. This was a "class" tournament. The buy-in was $10,000. I watched as the shoe came to one animated fellow. He bet $8,000, the maximum allowed under the tournament's rules.

He lost.

He was now sitting with less than $2,000. Most of the other players had their initial $10,000 and then some.

End of story? Don't bet on it.

When the game ended, our daring player won the $200,000 first prize.

Remember Chris Becker's comment: "A man isn't dead until his ass is cold"?

Remembering this, I wasn't discouraged after losing both of my large bets. I was low man on the totem pole. I had less than $1,200 in front of me. But my determination to win was as strong as ever.

Slowly, I won back small amounts of money until I had $2,600. The shoe came to me.

For some reason not entirely clear to me, tournament players look humiliated when they tap out and must leave the table while the tournament is still being played. I had no such qualms. If I lose, I leave with a smile.

I took my entire $2,600 and bet it on the Bank side. I dealt and won. I now had $5,200.

I bet the maximum allowed, $5,000, on the next hand. I won. I bet $5,000 again and won. I bet $5,000 again and won. I cut my wager to $2,000 and won. I now had $17,200.

I bet $1,200 and Player won, so I lost. I had $16,000. That was the 29th hand. At this point everyone had to pay Bank commissions and the supervisors announced the total chips held by each contestant. I had $14,800.

I was leader of the pack. But two players were each only a few thousand dollars behind me. The next (last) hand would decide the winner. How much to bet and on which side?

The dealer running the game announced, "The next hand will be the last hand of this shoe. It will be a secret wager."

This meant, as I explained earlier that you wrote your bet on a small slip of white paper. This was checked and initialed by a dealer and then folded so the others couldn't see it and placed it in front of you. If the two who were chasing me bet on Bank, I would have to bet enough so that if Bank won, they couldn't catch up.

On the last hand of the shoe, I usually bet Player. For reasons no mathematician can explain (for baccarat is a heads-or-tails game) Player seems to come up more often than Bank on both the first and the last hands. Veteran players tend to bet Player and Tie on the last hand.

THE PLAYERS TOOK a great deal of time figuring what to do. I kept hearing the Caller announce, "This will be the last hand of the shoe" and suddenly got the strong hunch that these two experienced players would bet on Player. The fact is that it *wasn't* the last hand of the shoe—it was the 30th hand. It was the last hand of the tournament. A shoe has 80 to 85 hands including ties. So I bet $4,700 on Bank and $100 (the maximum allowed) on tie.

Sure enough, as it later turned out when the secret wager slips were unfolded and announced, the two players closest to me in winnings made large bets on Player.

The shoe passed to the man on my right. He dealt two cards to Player. A five and a king for a total of 5. He peeked under his Bank cards, one at a time. "What would you like?" he asked me. "Stop wasting time," I said. "Turn over the natural eight." He was Italian but this time he peeked the way many Asians do, peering at each card from each of its four sides. "Would you take a natural nine?" he asked.

"An 8 is fine," I joked. "Nine would be overkill."

He peeked again. "Sorry," he said. Then he turned over a four and a five.

WITH THAT HAND I won the $106,000 first prize (the casino withheld $36,000 for taxes and so I was actually given $70,000). In addition, I had more than $19,000 in chips for additional winnings of $16,000. All told, my tournament win in the three levels plus the First Prize was just over $125,000.

Carole rushed into the baccarat pit amid cheers and excitement as champagne was brought out and photographs were taken. I must have shaken fifty hands before we left the casino the next day, Sunday, at noon. (Oh yes, on Sunday morning I won another $15,000 at the tables.)

NOT ALL TOURNAMENTS have happy endings. Just two weeks later I played in a tournament at another Atlantic City casino. This was a "winner take all" contest with $100,000 as the only prize.

There would be only two rounds. Each would consist of 40 deals. On the first round, I built my $500 buy-in to nearly $1,200. I was far ahead of the pack when the 40th (final) hand was announced.

Once again, we were required to make a secret bet. I bet $260 on Bank so that whichever way the hand went, and even if those closest to me bet the maximum $500 allowed, I would still have a $100 lead over them. I wagered $60 on Tie as an afterthought.

Three "desperadoes" at the other end of the table, having $500 or less and seeing no way to catch up, each bet $100 (the maximum allowed) on Tie. Tie is not a great wager: it pays 8-to-1, but the chances of its coming up are less than one-in-twelve.

Sure enough, the improbable happened. The final hand was a 6-6 Tie and those three knocked me out—for all my careful play!

After that, almost nothing went right. At a *Megabucks* slot machine I got three *Megabucks* in a row on the bottom line. These paid $10. A fourth Megabucks on the same line would have given me $7,100,000 over a 20-year period!

43

THE BACCARAT SHOE

Just as a monkey could throw dice, a barking seal could be trained to deal a baccarat shoe. Nevertheless, we're all human and get strong feelings about other people. If we don't care for someone's look or style, we tend to bet against them. If we like em, we sometimes bet with em even against our own strong instincts!

When a shoe is passed to you and Player has won the previous three hands, you *must* bet Player. You'll win as often as you lose. The fact that you're holding the shoe doesn't change the face of a single card in it. (God has not taken time out from counting the proceeds in the big collection plate in the sky to look down and turn that Queen of Spades into a Nine of Clubs because you once were a Boy Scout.)

So, even though it "goes against your grain"—bet Player. It need only be a small bet. If you lose, you'll still have the shoe and then you can bet Bank.

If it is psychologically impossible for you to bet against yourself while you're dealing, then simply pass the shoe this time.

Keep in mind that the improbable happens and that gaming results are often a paradox. What do you do if you know that an average shoe ends with thirty-four Bank wins and thirty-one Player wins, and now the shoe has shown forty-five Player wins and there are about four hands left?

I know clever fellows who would respond: "I'd bet heavily on Bank catching up."

It could. And then again maybe it won't.

I go with the trend. If Player has come up 45 times, it could come up 5 more.

IN THIS TOME, as I explained in the beginning, I didn't burden you with rules. I assume that you know them—or can pick them up with ease elsewhere. But for the Mr. Machados among you, let me say of baccarat that the game is so simple as to seem silly. Perhaps it is its stark simplicity that has kept it going for more than five hundred years.

It's a game of nines. You want the side you bet on to have a total of 9—or as close to it as possible. Eight is better than seven; seven better than six, etc.

The person holding the shoe deals two cards to the Player and two to himself. They're dealt face down but it wouldn't affect results—only suspense—if they were dealt face up.

WHEN EITHER HAND has a 2-card total of 8 or 9 (called naturals), the hand is over—no one draws a third card. 9 beats 8 and ties are standoffs where neither side wins or loses.

The Player is first to act and will always draw a third card having a hand total of 0, 1, 2, 3, 4, or 5. With 8 or 7 the Player stands.

When the Player draws or stays, the Bank automatically draws to 0, 1 and 2. When the Player stands with a total of 6 or 7, the Bank draws having 0, 1, 2, 3, 4, 5, stands having 6 or 7.

With a count of 3, 4, 5, 8, whether the Bank draws a third card or stands is determined by the face value of the third card the Player draws.

If the Bank has a count of 3, he draws a third card only when dealing 1, 2, 3, 4, 5, 6, 7, 9, 10 as the Player third card. He does not draw when dealing an 8.

If the Bank has a count of 4, he draws a third card only when dealing a 2, 3, 4, 5, 6, 7 as the Player third card. He does not draw when dealing a 1, 8, 9, 10.

If the Bank has a count of 5, he draws when dealing a 4, 5, 6, 7 as the Player third card. He does not draw when dealing a 1, 2, 3, 8, 9, 10.

And when the Bank has a count of 6, he draws only when dealing a 6 or 7 as the Player third card. He does not draw when dealing any other card. The Bank always stands having 7.

Pictures and tens count as zero. Since the goal is 9, a total of 10 counts for zero. Thus 6 and 5 add up to 1 while 3 and 9 add up to 2.

EVERY CASINO HAS, free for the asking, a card that explains the rules.

But, as you must have grasped by now, you don't have to know the rules!

The table has three dealers. Two are seated and take care of paying and collecting bets, collecting commissions on winning Bank bets, making change, and exchanging chips for cash or markers.

The third man or woman, the Caller, stands and directs the player dealing from the shoe. He calls for the initial cards. Then he announces the totals for each side. He requests a further card for either or both sides if the rules call for it. He announces the winner.

The cards lie there, face up on the table, until all wagers are settled.

BACCARAT GIVES some Las Vegas Strip casinos about 12 percent of their profits. These from a comparatively few players.

Not bad?

I don't know any other casino game that can so frighten gambling bosses. The game can win big money but it can also lose it.

The Aladdin once lost a quarter of a million dollars to three winners in three days, and closed the game for three months.

Another casino installed a larger shoe and dealt a shoe containing sixteen decks instead of the usual eight.* It kept its maximum bet limit at $2,000. It was running scared. If

---

*One reason for this may be that casinos know that when a shoe is ended, players tend to leave. That's "get away" time. Commissions are settled and people get up to stretch, go to the washrooms, etc. The notion that by doubling the decks you'll keep em longer may seem sound, but isn't. People need an occasional rest. A casino on Fremont Street once experimented with the longest shoe in the world: 144 decks. It was amusing to watch, but few took it seriously and the shoe was eventually removed.

you wanted the right to bet $4,000, they told you you need-
ed to have $25,000 cash on deposit in its cage.

None of this has ever been explained logically to me by
any casino executive. A wager is a wager. What difference
if your first bet is $100 and your next $4,000? The casino
has the same per against on every wager. Is it fear that
someone will wager $25, $50, $100, $200, $500, $1,000,
$2,000, $4,000, $8,000, $10,000 in that sequence?

If they lost three bets and won the fourth, they'd win
$25. If they lost the first seven and won the eighth, they win
$125. Or if they lost nine and won the tenth (maximum)
$10,000 wager, the player would have dropped $5,875 plus
Bank commissions if the win was on the Bank side.

44

ATTITUDE IS (ALMOST) EVERYTHING

Tommy Renzoni insisted to me that when someone he knew came in and sat at the table, he could tell after just a few hands whether that person would be a winner or loser for the session.

It didn't matter, insisted Tommy, whether the player won or lost those first few bets. It was just something about him. Attitude.

Tommy and I once sat in Gramercy Park in Manhattan where he talked about his dream. He wanted to open a really classy baccarat casino. Nothing but baccarat. Large minimums. Large maximums.

He wanted the place open only from 10 P.M. until 4 A.M.

"But Tommy," I said, "Las Vegas is a 24-hour town. Everybody else is open around-the-clock."

Tommy looked at me with his soft wide eyes.

"Lyle," he said, "I've been in gambling all of my life. Nobody is ever going to play with my money while I'm asleep!"

Although Tommy supervised the game at the Sands and saw numerous fortunes lost, he himself was a prisoner of the gaming fever. He would gather a stake of $30,000 and hurry over to Caesars Palace—where he generally lost.

Once he won $42,000 and suffered a slight heart attack. He was rushed to the hospital. The next evening he got up from his bed, dressed himself, signed himself out of the hospital in front of two bewildered nurses and an intern, and taxied to Caesars Palace. There, he quickly dropped the $42,000.

Tommy never saw his dream come true. When Howard Hughes bought the Sands at a-sell-it-to-me-today-or-not-at-all bargain price, the skimming stopped. And Tommy, forced to live on only his salary and a share of the tokes (tips), couldn't quite adjust.

He quit.

He moved to Circus Circus and in the Baccarat pit he introduced the game of Barbooth. It originated in Greece and is a dead-even game. One player tosses three dice from a white cup and another throws three dice from a black cup. The house takes 5 percent from the winner, giving it a healthy 2.5 percent profit.

Tommy's high hopes for the game crashed when players found it boring. The rules required too many tosses of dice to reach a decision. Baccarat is a game where every hand is a decision—a decision that can take less than one minute to arrive at.

When Tommy's wife died of cancer, he lost the will to live. A short time after her death, he visited a friend at the Tropicana and complained about how he couldn't shake the depression he felt about the loss.

Then he went outside and walked in front of a speeding car. He was killed instantly.

Today his son, Tommy Renzoni, Jr., works as a dealer on a Mississippi riverboat casino. And for a long time, there were few baccarat games in Las Vegas which didn't have one or more of "Tommy's boys"—the crew that worked with him in the original Sands game.

FRANK SINATRA was no hero to baccarat dealers. He was noisy and he was rude. He made demands that he knew the dealers weren't allowed to meet. He seemed to take pleasure in insulting casino employees.

Frankie-boy had an $8,000-a-hand limit at Caesars Palace but kept insisting that he wanted $16,000. He would often hold up the game, hand after hand, insisting on the right to bet $16,000.

Instructions were very firm. Sinatra was not to be dealt cards unless he announced his intentions.

"Mr. Sinatra, are you shilling or going for the money?"

He balked at answering. Too often he played and, after a loss, stood up and said he was "only fooling" which meant he was "shilling" for the casino and not obligated to pay the loss.

Once, over a few-week period, Sinatra and Beverly Hills real estate broker Danny Schwartz won more than one million dollars from Caesars Palace. They collected every penny.

Now, Sinatra, doing a solo, was losing it back rapidly. But instead of cash he was papering the cage with markers.

On the fateful night I'm about to describe, instructions were issued to limit Sinatra's credit to $400,000.

He reached that point though he still had a handful of white*($500) chips on the table in front of him. He kept insisting he wanted another $25,000.

The croupier summoned casino boss, Sanford Waterman. Sandy, usually cool and wise, ordinarily would have sent security men to the troubled baccarat pit. Instead, he hurried over himself.

"Frank," he explained, "you owe us four hundred big ones. If you want more you've got to give us something. The boys want their money."

Sinatra stood up. He flung his white chips into Sandy Waterman's face, at the same time smacking him on the forehead with the palm of his hand.

Waterman spun about and ran to his room. Within minutes he returned with a loaded pistol in hand. He pointed it at the singer.

"Listen you! If you ever lay a hand on me again I'll put a bullet through your head!"

Sanford Waterman had indeed lost his cool.

Sinatra didn't lose his. "Aw, come on," he said with a disparaging tone of voice, "that gun stuff went out with Humphrey Bogart!"

Disconcerted by Sinatra's nonchalant response, Waterman's lowered his arm just enough for one of Sinatra's gofers to strike it. The pistol fell to the floor. Waterman knew he was in trouble. He turned and raced to the cashier cage, with Sinatra and his wolf pack racing after him in hot pursuit.

---

*For trivia fans: during that time $500 chips were white and $1,000 chips were yellow. Today, in most casinos, $500 chips are purple and $1,000 chips are orange.

It so happened that, at the time, Sinatra's left arm was in a sling, the result of some surgery on his veins. The cashier cage door opened. Waterman tried to close it behind him but Sinatra clung to it. The door smashed back against his bandaged arm. Blood spurted upward. Everyone stood appalled. The drama was over as Sinatra hurried to his third floor suite and a gofer went for the house doctor.

The baccarat scene is never dull.

BACCARAT

B	P	B	P	B	P	B	P
	X		X		X	X	
X		X		X		X	
	X		X		X	X	
X			X		X		X
	X	X			X		X
	X	X		X		X TIE	
	X	X			X	X	
X			X	X	X TIE		X
	X		X	X	TIE		X
	X	X	X	X			X
TIE			X	X			X
X			X		X		X
X			X	X		TIE	X
X			X	X	X		X
X			X	X	X		X
X			X	X	X	TIE	X
	X	X	TIE		X		X
X		X	TIE		X TIE		
	X	X			X		
	X	X		X			

45

KEEPING YOUR
BACCARAT SCORECARD

This is a scorecard. You simply ask for one. They're available at every baccarat pit in the world.

In 1977, most players kept score similar to that shown on the left.

I REQUIRED MORE information than that. So, I developed my own system. I came armed with both red and black pens. I numbered the decisions and I used black for a lost bet, and red for a winning bet. Black, circled, indicates a hand on which I didn't bet.

Ties are indicated by a flat line.

On the next page is a reproduction of the results of a shoe I played. I've selected a winning card with a not untypical run of decisions.

Note that I played only 66 of the 76 hands. Note, too, that I won 33 and lost 31 of those the 64. In other words, I won just two more than I lost.—Yet when the shoe ended I was $11,600 ahead on this one.

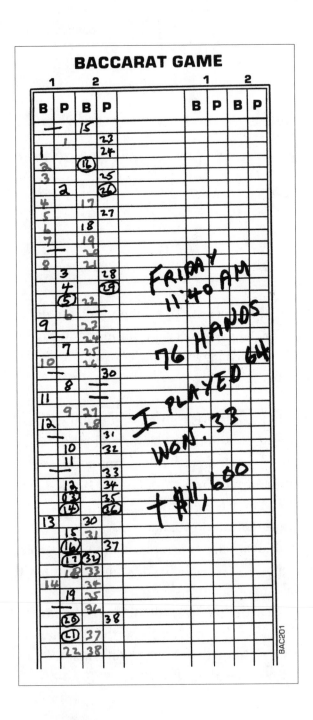

I EXPLAINED MY score-keeping system in *Casino Gambling for the Winner,* which was published in 1978. In those days, the casino provided you only with a card and a lead pencil. Today, the majority of casinos offer you pens or pencils with one end in blue and the other in red. (If I could have patented my idea and collected a royalty on two-color pencils and pens I'd be able to cruise forever on the *Crystal Harmony!*)

YOU MUST HAVE a plan or strategy. You must decide how much money you will risk; how much you want to win; how long you will play.

Money and time management are the keys that will open the only doors that lead to winning.

As I explained earlier, I usually limit myself to two complete shoes. Interestingly enough, and because I'm not in harmony with what's happening on balance, I tend to lose more than I win when I sit down and play partial shoes. I've learned that for me, at least, it pays to be patient.

Nor do I ever play baccarat without keeping a score-card.

HERE'S ANOTHER of those cases where I didn't quite practice what I preach.

I went to a baccarat table at the old MGM Grand in Las Vegas. The only players were shills. I told the supervisor I'd wait until they played a new shoe. This shoe looked to have another ten minutes to go. The casino doesn't make money from shills so, in defeat, the dealers were directed to stop the charade and shuffle the cards for a new shoe.

I played two complete shoes. I had arrived at McCarran Airport from New York at 11:15 A.M., and when the second shoe ended, it was 1:30 P.M. I glanced at my wristwatch. I had plenty of time to catch a flight back to New York.

Terrific!

I counted my chips. I was $23,250 ahead.

Then there occurred one of those freak encounters— the kind that only seem to happen to gamblers. A stranger sat down next to me while the dealers were shuffling the cards for a new shoe that I didn't intend to play.

"Damn!" he exclaimed.

Quite naturally I asked, "What's the matter?"

"Oh, hell! I'm supposed to catch a plane to New York and it's been delayed two hours."

I knew he was talking about my flight. I knew also and straight away that I wasn't going to permit this information to keep me at the table. In all of Las Vegas of all the baccarat tables this fellow had to sit next to and share his troubles with me!

Had he not sat down, I would have driven to the airport, turned in my Hertz car, and happily sat in the lounge reading magazines, newspapers and books to pass the two hours.

I went to a public phone. Yes, said the lady at the other end of the phone, my flight was delayed. It wouldn't depart until 4:30.

I reserved a First Class seat. (On this one-stop trip I was picking up my own airfare and it had been deducted before I figured my winnings.)

I hurried out of the casino to the shopping arcade. I had my photograph taken with "Leo, the MGM lion" for $15. Then I went to my rented automobile and sped downtown to one of the small joints that advertise payoffs of 98 percent on slots. It took me fifteen minutes to get rid of $2 worth of nickels and ten minutes to get rid of $20 in Eisenhower dollars. I was time-passing and euphoric.

I played some dice. The house had a $100 limit including odds. I played blackjack. $50 limit. Suddenly, without seeming to, I had pissed away $740.

I was annoyed with myself. I got in the car again and started for the airport. I struggled against the urge to stop off at a "regular" casino and win it back.

I lost the struggle and pulled into the Stardust.

They were mixing a new shoe. It was afternoon and I was the only real player. I bet $800 on the first deal. I won.

I won the next three bets.

I lost 9 of the next 11. When I stood up I had lost all the cash in my pocket.

Do not despair, dear reader—all the cash wasn't all the money I had won.

This time I controlled the urge to pull into another casino to win back my new larger loss.

At the airport I counted my money. Deducting all expenses, I was still $14,250 ahead.

Which brings us to the subject of money management, except that first I want to show you the two MGM cards.

Note that on the two cards combined there were 138 hands dealt, not counting 17 ties.

Of these I played 114. Of these I won 66.

That's better than half. However, I must point out that often I win fewer than half the hands I bet and still walk away a big money winner.

There isn't a lot of rhyme or reason to the play you see here except that you should observe that at no time did I buck a trend of three or more. On the contrary, note on the second card, I bet and lost three times in a row against Player. My choice then was either to bet Player or not to bet at all.

I switched to Player and won the next six hands.

What follows is my money strategy at baccarat.

I'll talk in terms of my numbers and you can translate these down (or up) into your own money amounts.

I bet $4,000. If I win, I take the winnings and reduce my wager to $2,000. Now, win or lose I'm $2,000 ahead.

If I win the second time, I play for $2,500. Then $3,000. Then $3,500.

With five successive winning bets I have won $15,000 on Player. On Bank it is $15,000 less the "commission" of $750, or a net profit of $14,250.

Sequences of 5 don't come up that often. (Look back at my 144 game record.) Nevertheless, they do come up.

At this point I often drop down to $2,000 again. Or $1,000. I'm not greedy. I'm willing to have the stake build up again if I'm into one of those 7 or 8 or 10 sequences!

Okay. Let's imagine I'm playing Bank. If I lose the first bet, I lost $4,000.

If I win one but lose the second, I'm ahead a net of $1,800.

If I win two bets but lose the third bet, I'm ahead $3,200.

If I win three bets but lose the fourth bet, I'm ahead $5,075.

If I win four bets but lose the fifth bet, I'm ahead $7,425.

If I'm bold and win 5 in a row and stay with $3,500 for the 6th and lose that one, I'm still ahead $10,750. If I win and get off, I'm ahead $17,575.

Should I win that one, it's $4,000 a hand all the way with the clear understanding that the house is going to win the final bet—the one I lose.

Let's try a variation. Instead of an initial wager of $4,000, you bet $1,000. Then $2,000. Then $4,000.

You are really wagering that whichever side you are betting with will win one out of three. In which case you will be $1,000 ahead on the Player's side and $950 on the Bank side—depending on which way you've bet.

You're also risking $7,000 with which to do it. Ain't nothing certain in life. You can lose $7,000.

Let's break it down further. Let's make an initial bet of $500. Then $1,000. Then $2,000. Then $4,000. You're now betting $7,500 against the other side having a run of four consistent winning hands. You stand to profit $500 on Player, less on Bank.

Let's extend your chance (and violate my "Rule of Three") by waiting for either side to win two in a row and then starting to bet the other side. Now you're really wagering that the other side won't win six times in a row.

Sometimes shoe after shoe will be dealt out without either Bank or Player winning six hands in a row.

(I should mention in passing that in the days before people kept scorecards, players were not as conscious of

Player winning runs. Thus, if someone held the shoe for a while, everyone would be aware that Bank made 3 and then 4 and then 5 passes. But when Player won hand after hand and the shoe moved around the table, people were less conscious of the fact that Player had won 6 or 7 in a row.)

No matter how lucky you are, and no matter how fortunate your runs or your guesses, you won't be lucky forever.

Lesson to be learned: grab your winnings and run!

46

MANAGING YOUR MONEY

Money management is your key to making it. There are many and contrasting points of view on how this should be done. Here are tips based on my own experience.

1. If you carry cash, keep most of it in a safe deposit box. In modern hotels there will be a safe in your room. If not, safekeeping is available (without charge) at the cashier's cage or at the hotel's front desk. As you win, return to the box and deposit at least a portion of your winnings. Get the cash out of your possession and into the strongbox as quickly as you can. Go to the box as often as you need to for this purpose. Having your money locked away is one hedge against letting the gaming fever get you. Even the inconvenience of returning to the box for more money can cool you off. There are too many times when weariness will cause you to spring for (and lose) all the cash on your person.

292 ♣ WINNING ♦ AT ♥ CASINO ♠ GAMBLING

2. Set a firm credit limit and instruct the casino credit manager flatly and firmly to note on your card that if more credit is extended to you than the maximum you've requested, you won't pay the excess. They won't love you for it, and they'll hate me for telling you this but the credit manager, as charming as he or she may be (and many are charmers), is not your best friend. Though happy to bury you, it's doubtful if she or he'd take time to be one of the pallbearers.

THERE IS A PLOY in Vegas called "stretch and break." When a credit manager sees that you've put a limit of $5,000 or $10,000 or $20,000 on your credit and knows that you'd probably be good for $30,000 or $40,000 or $50,000, he sometimes feels that his job is to extend your credit. Ask and thou shalt receive.

Greed operates on both sides of the table.

Don't fall into the quagmire of extending your credit. Harold S. Smith, Jr., who, with his father, owned Harolds Club in Reno, advised against ever writing checks. He believed in carrying enough cash to play with (even depositing it in the cashier's cage and playing against it to show them you're serious) and if that goes, you go.

I've known people who went to casino areas for the sunshine. They didn't plan to gamble. But each morning they had to traverse the casino to reach the newspaper stand. The newspaper cost them an average of $50 a day.

Then there is the classic story about the late great Joe E. Lewis. He was a very funny comedian and a very compulsive gambler.

Joe was dining with an attractive chorine. She asked him to get her some cigarettes. He couldn't find a cigarette girl in the restaurant so he left the table and obligingly hurried through the casino to the notions counter in the lobby. He returned in a few minutes with her cigarettes.

When the meal was over, Lewis noticed that the young lady was about to leave the open pack on the table.

"Better take these with you, honey," he said. "They cost me $32,000."

And it wasn't part of his comedy routine.

It happens that way all the time. A compulsive friend will drop a bankroll between dessert and coffee while supposedly making a phone call or visiting the gent's room.

Colonel* Tom Parker was Elvis Presley's manager. He was also a born loser in casinos. I watched him play roulette and craps and he was a sucker for those odds-against-you proposition bets at craps.

I once knew a few turkeys to cost him one hundred thousand dollars. He was about to check out of the Aladdin in Las Vegas to fly to Palm Springs. In the lobby he remarked to the hotel manager that the turkey the hotel served the night before had been particularly tasty. Elvis and he had really enjoyed it.

"Would you like some to take with you?" casino manager Gil Gilbert asked. "We've got some freshly roasted."

The Colonel was known as a fellow who never turned down a freebie.

---

*I assume he's a fellow Kentucky Colonel. Shortly after *Casino Gambling for the Winner* was published I received a call from the Kentucky Governor's office asking if I'd like him to make me a Kentucky Colonel. I agreed and so each year, at Kentucky Derby time, I'm invited to a barbecue for the Kentucky Colonels just before Derby Day.

I've yet to set foot in Kentucky.

"Sure thing," he replied.

While waiting for the kitchen staff to pack four turkeys, the Colonel wandered into the casino and dropped one hundred big ones at craps.

His name on credit cards and at the tables was "Mr. Snow." And he was a lollipop for the free things in life. He would ask for a free box of cigars after having dropped a quarter of a million dollars—enough to buy his own small cigar factory.

Just after Elvis's death the word around was that the real reason the semi-retired singer had started working full-time again was to help the Colonel pay off some of his casino markers.

47

WHERE TO PLAY

Casinos have personalities. You will have subjective feelings about various casinos. Some will seem cold and distant. Others warm and friendly.

There are many large casinos in the world and obviously you won't be able to play in all of them.

Which one(s) do you choose?

I'm reminded of a funny routine that iconoclastic comedian Lenny Bruce used to perform. He talked about "good rooms for performers."

"They say that the Waldorf-Astoria has a good room," Bruce would remark. "Well, if the Waldorf-Astoria offered me $10,000 a week and the men's room at the YMCA offered me $10,001—I'll be at the YMCA like that! *That's* a good room!"

The best casino? The one with the best food? The best shows? The sexiest cocktail waitresses? The most cordial casino personnel? The best tennis courts and/or golf courses?

Sure. For Samson Sucker and Dolly Dope.

Not for you, pal. *You're not there for the niceties.* You're there to win money! (Try to hold on to that thought!)

Therefore, *ipso facto,* the best casino is the casino where you win the most.

Repeat after me: "The best casino is where I win!"

Elementary? Not at all. Years ago when I held the record as the worst poker player in the world, I watched Jerry Jacobs, one of the best poker players I knew. When he was in action, he was so good that we nicknamed him "the Butcher"—for he carved the rest of us up. Most of us were at the game for the sociability and the fun. Not so the Butcher. He was there for the money. He was pleasant and gracious—but not for one moment did he forget why he was there. It was pleasure for us, an income-producing business for him.

Watching him taught me why I could never be a top-notch poker winner. When someone at the table was a large loser, I measured my bets accordingly. I was reluctant to pile woes upon woes.

Not the Butcher. He explained it to me succinctly. "Who are you most likely to take money from? The losers, of course. So you must go after losers with a vengeance."

It sounds logical. Apply it to casino gambling and the directive would seem apparent, yes? Watch the people you know. Again and again they will return to those casinos where they are steady losers—where they're so unlucky that even the postage stamp vending machine in the lobby doesn't work for them. Again and again they will try to "win back" from or "best" those casinos where they consistently lose their money.

That casino where they won some bucks? Sure, they'll play there occasionally. But the real challenge is head-to-head against that place that already has (too much of) "their" money.

It's like the proverbial moth feeding itself into the flame.

Control yourself. When you consistently run unlucky at any casino, *accept the fact that that casino isn't a lucky place for you.*

Don't fight it. Simply avoid it. But avoid it like a plague. And if you find yourself being tempted to "give it another try" then it's time to get out of town.

You must be alert at all times. The minute you lose sight of your goals—the minute you take your mind off your purpose—you risk becoming a victim of your own human frailty—that self-destructive instinct in all of us which lies just beneath the surface.

Don't write checks that you didn't plan to write. And don't sign markers that you wouldn't be signing if you hadn't lingered too long.

CASINOS THRIVE for more reasons than those mathematical percentages against you. They have an additional percentage in the human factor. Don't gift them with this one!

48

THE GAMBLING DEMON

The first people to make serious studies of gaming were economists and they were confounded by the notion that gambling is a losing proposition and therefore irrational.

This conclusion was challenged by William Vickery in 1945. Vickery said that gaming should be measured not by expected money gains but because the money a gambler doesn't have may seem more valuable to him than what he has. He was supported by Alex Rubner, who wrote: "... gambling can be rational when non-pecuniary pleasure or sensations are desired; gambling as an economic goal is only rational when a person's wish to obtain an otherwise unattainable large lump is very strong. Thus gambling for a poor man may be rational[*]."

Here is what some other "experts" have to say on the subject:

L. Monroe Starkey has reported that "Gaming is symptomatic of deeper distresses in our social structure—

[*]Source: *The Economics of Gambling* by Alex Rubner, published in London.

tedious and purposeless occupations, inequitable distribution of the nation's wealth, cheap and inconsistent law enforcement, the Horatio Alger myth of success by sweat in the face of insurmountable economic and social obstacles, the continued stress on personal initiative to the neglect of community responsibility."

The usual view of gambling is that it is destructive to the individual, undermines the work ethic, and removes money from the legitimate marketplace. More recent research developed some less rigid views. For example, the proposition that people gamble beyond their means was disputed as unproved, and the claim that gambling is detrimental to society was countered by the argument that gambling is an outlet for frustrations, a relief from loneliness, and a leveler of class distinction.

Some psychological theorists regard gambling as a normal form of recreation, destructive only to those who become addicted to it or get involved in its criminal aspects. In the case of addiction, they claim, the proper solution is to cure the addict and not condemn gambling per se.

The person who visits a casino for the recreation is easy prey for the casino operator. Everywhere he'll be invited to win automobiles, boats, and huge jackpots.

When a jackpot is hit on a slot machine, bells ring, lights flash and often the win is announced over a loudspeaker.

The prestige-seeking drives of a player are catered to by expensive, ostentatious architecture and decor, and the desire for recreational fun is filled by swimming pools, golf courses, shows, shops, and, of course, games. The casinos also appeal to the competitive instincts of a gambler. In Blackjack, for example, the player is pitted against the dealer, one-to-one, and the battle is usually witnessed by a gallery of his peers. In Baccarat, it's the man with the shoe against the man who bets Player.

A Las Vegas psychiatrist, Irving Katz, has suggested that gambling can be meaningful in a person's life because that person lacks satisfactory personal relationships. Katz said: "Many people are alienated and lonely. I find this among compulsive as well as social gamblers. They are not getting enough out of life, they are not getting contact out of life. They feel powerless. In gambling they have a sense of power. A turn of a card, the roll of the dice, the spin of a roulette wheel gives them a feeling that they are some-what controlling their lives and luck is on their side."

Do you recall your first gambling experience? For many, it took place in their pre-teen days. They attended a church bingo game with Mom or at a church carnival, Dad watched while they tossed baseballs at milk bottles to win a Cupie doll. The beginnings are innocent.

You don't have to attend a Gamblers Anonymous meeting to learn about the damage done to man and women by casinos. No less an authority than the late Hank Greenspun, the courageous publisher of the *Las Vegas Sun*, wrote:

> Public officials considering the legalization of gambling in various states should sit in the editor's chair at the *Las Vegas Sun* and hear the stories of those whom gambling has harmed. This would include every legitimate merchant, owners of rental hous-

ing, and lending institutions that provide money for home purchases.

Families have been deprived of proper food and have been unable to pay rents and mortgages because of gambling losses. Along the lines of the Surgeon General's warning on cigarette packs, those in lower income groups should be warned that gambling can become an addiction.

I HAVE INCLUDED this "downer" material in these pages because nobody says you *have to* gamble. Nor does anybody say you have to lose. There is no law limiting your thought process.

You've got a mind of your own and you must let it take charge. It must grapple with temptation to discard the rules of the game as they're set out in this book. It must be clear and calm and it must constantly churn enough perspective into your thinking so that when the going is bad, you'll accept that reality and take a walk.

I SAID EARLY ON that gamblers were crazy. Gambling is crazy. If you can't or won't stick to a series of strict attitudes, then give up the casinos and take up crossword puzzles or cribbage.

49

THE ROAD TO VICTORY

If by this time in the book you don't feel completely win-oriented, then it's time to ask yourself again:

"Do I *really* want to win?"

If the answer isn't a clear affirmative, read this slowly and carefully!

What makes a compulsive gambler?

"Emotional immaturity," says a California psychologist.

Like the chronic alcoholic, the compulsive gambler is rebellious, self-centered, and ultimately self-destructive. His or her anti-social attitudes create feelings of guilt. That sense of guilt can be allayed only by punishment. Thus, the compulsive gambler secretly wishes to lose.

Increased opportunities because of the rapid birth of new casinos are contributing to an accelerated rate of abusive gambling. I wrote this book for would-be winners—not losers. But you should be alert to the signs of compulsive gambling behavior.

304 ♣ WINNING ♦ AT ♥ CASINO ♠ GAMBLING

RONALD A. ROSTON, of the University of California at Los Angeles, at an annual meeting of the American Psychological Association in Chicago, declared "The compulsive gambler unconsciously strives to recreate and confirm infantile feelings of omnipotence by rebelling against the realities of conventional society. His rebellion, manifested in gambling, arouses guilt; by losing, he expiates guilt."

Are *you* a compulsive gambler?

If you gamble more than you can comfortably afford to lose, tend to plunge when you are behind, and just can't quit when you know you should, the answer is probably *yes*.

They tell tales of a heroin addict so desperate that he will punch his own mother in the mouth to knock her teeth out so he can sell the gold in them for a fix.

No level of society is immune. I knew of a banker who used to lose big and had his bank's armored car drive to the casino with cash so he could pay off his markers. The trouble was that the money was bank money. The banker soon got his long-needed rest-cure in the penitentiary.

A word about markers.

I've told you how to limit yourself. If you don't put rigid bars against going above your set limit and if your record of paying off is good, the casino will cheerfully help you on your way to bankruptcy. They'll stop just short of knocking out your teeth for the gold.

In the heat of play you'll sign anything to get more money. Casinos will ask you to sign a "retraction slip" saying that you are asking for more credit and want to cancel the previous limit.

Don't.

That's a simple enough instruction, yes?

Don't.

If your credit is good and your intentions are good, there is plenty of time to pay off markers.

If the casino has tried to stretch and break you (allowed you to exceed your established limit) you can be a big sport* and pay them off, when you can. Or you can settle for a partial payment.

I know one floorman who is decades ahead of his own bosses in his thinking. His feeling about good players who reach the point where they can't pay off their markers is that they will come to town anyway, but avoid the casinos where they owe money.

His philosophy is that after two years, when most unpaid markers are considered worthless (uncollectable), he would write the markers off and mail them back to the customer with a Christmas card saying, "We appreciate your *cash* business."

No more credit, but let them come back to where they're known and comfortable and drop their money in friendly surroundings.

But this isn't going to be you.

---

*Read that word as "sucker."

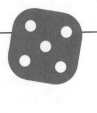

50

BITS AND PIECES

I f you play for serious money, whether it be Atlantic City, Minnesota, an American Indian reservation, or Vegas or Reno, the casino will be your host. If you have a $10,000 card, your room, food and drink should be compliments of the house. Atlantic City casinos should send a limousine for you and Nevada casinos should pick up the tab for one coach fare.

$20,000 should entitle you to bring a friend and the casino will pick up two fares. $25,000 or more should entitle you to two First Class plane tickets from New York and almost everything comped. Almost—because they aren't going to hand you unlimited cash—so such cash items as valet service, tips and phone calls have to be picked up by you.

Don't forget to stop off at the cashier's window and settle your incidentals bill when you're checking out. With many hotels completely on computer, I know of a case where a medium-stakes player was told his credit was no longer good when he tried to book a junket. He had been prompt enough in paying casino markers, but he owed $6 for dry cleaning which he hadn't paid before he departed. When he received a statement for the $6 from the hotel, he ignored it.

Before I give you the casino's philosophy, let me ask if you know the one about the man who was about to commit suicide by leaping into Boulder Dam.

He was a junior bank executive and he had swindled one hundred thousand dollars from his bank—all of which he'd lost at blackjack. The bank examiners were due the next·day, and when he confessed the whole thing to his wife, she packed her things and left him.

Suddenly he heard a voice call, "Don't jump, Sonny! There is no need to end your life! I'm a witch and I can help you."

He turned around to see a wrinkled old lady dressed in black, smiling, with some front teeth missing.

"I doubt it," he told her sadly. "I've stolen a hundred grand from the bank, for which I'll probably be arrested tomorrow, and my wife just left me."

"Young man, witches can fix anything," she said. "I'm going to perform a witch miracle." Then she looked heavenward and said: "Alakazam! The hundred thousand dollars has been replaced and, in addition, there's an extra hundred thousand in your safe deposit box! Alakazam! Your wife is home again waiting for you!"

He looked at her in disbelief, "Is all this true?" he asked.

"Of course," she said, "but to validate it, you must do one thing."

"Anything!" he said. "Anything!"

"I'm horny. You must take me to a motel and have sexual intercourse with me."

He stared at her. She was as ugly as could be, dressed in rags. Nevertheless, he felt he had little choice. He agreed. He took a room in a nearby motel and screwed her all night. In the morning, as he was getting dressed and combing his hair in front of the mirror, she lay on the bed watching silently.

Finally, she asked, "Sonny, how old are you?"

"I'm thirty-two," he said.

"Tell me something, then," she asked. "Aren't you a little too old to believe in witches?"

AND, INDEED, dear reader, you are old enough to know there's no such a thing as something for nothing.

You pay dues, one way or another, for everything in life.

So, the casino doesn't have as its objective giving you its money as a birthday present. Not even when it's your birthday.

You are comped and your air fare is paid only because the casino values you as a source of profit for its business. The management assumes that if you stay at its hotel, you'll do most of your playing at its hotel. And leave most of your losses there, too.

They're taking a chance on you but it isn't much of a gamble. They know how much your fare comes to; that's a fixed amount. They can estimate from experience your cost to them in terms of room, food and drink bills.

I drink Diet-Pepsi. The next fellow wakens to champagne. The casino is willing to spring for 20 to 30 percent of what it expects to win from you. Thus, someone with a

$25,000 card who drops all or most of it on every visit can be comped with air fare and charges of up to $5,000 without making anyone unhappy.

Few players consume the full allowance. But the unused portion helps as a cushion against those limited few who come and win and leave winners.

51

THEY'RE WATCHING YOU

They're watching you!

The old-fashioned eye-in -the-sky consisted of a series of one-way mirrors on the casino ceiling. When the money was big, there was a chance that, in addition to all the observers you could see, there was another pair of eyes watching you from "up there."

Enter: modern technology. Merv Griffin's Resorts in Atlantic City led the way with a bank of 116 video recorders. Today, every modern casino has a video camera trained on every active table. Nevada casinos are required to have at least two cameras that can hone in on every table.

Tapes record the date, hour, and minute, as well as the identification number of the table. With a flick, a camera can zoom in so closely on a player or dealer that you can observe skin cells that even the naked human eye can't see.

I like that. I'm an honest player. I don't cheat and I don't want the casino to cheat me. That's my unspoken pact with them. Give me a fair chance at your money, and I'll give you a fair chance at mine.

It means that I don't play at little out-of-the-way clubs which could be hurt if I won because they need the money. It means the box men will see that no shaved dice come into the game. It means the blackjack pit boss will see that nobody deals seconds. I play only where I can take some money and still leave them smiling.

They don't always smile everywhere.

A few casinos have a tight-assed policy on credit and a very unhappy view of winners. They don't like to be did- dled by the dirty digit of destiny. They will, on occasion, ask you to leave.

Not for doing anything wrong. Nothing shady. Nothing crooked. Nothing sharp.

Just plain winning.

A cardinal sin. And one worthy of excommunication. Exclusion.

Remember now, I'm not talking about blackjack coun- ters. That question was settled favorably for counters play- ing in Atlantic City and, I believe, will in time be changed in Nevada.

I happen to believe it's much ado about nothing. The casino can make a new shoe at will. A dealer dealing from one or two decks can shuffle after every deal.

I'm talking about honest, albeit lucky players. I would think you should have the right to play anywhere, provid- ed you put your money up and conduct yourself in an orderly manner. Most casinos will let you strike it rich and know that eventually they'll recoup their money. You'll overstay your luck. You'll lose it back.

If you're a messenger and travel to another casino to lose it there, they'll console themselves with the hope that some day you'll win somewhere else and carry the money back to them.

If you are going to do high-stakes gambling you should confine it to resorts which are large and successful. Keep away from out-of-the-way casinos. Keep out of grind joints.

Now let me tell you something that I should have stressed earlier. Your job is to win and run, right?

The casino's job is to keep you playing. The longer you play the better their chances.

It's something called Decisions.

Decisions. Decisions. Decisions.

The house wants as many decisions as possible. For example, if the percentage on a game is 2, they need fifty decisions (in theory) to take 100 percent of your stake.

Some dealers will deal so fast that you may not have a moment to scratch your head.

Decisions!

You'll find the drive to decisions everywhere. Black-jack. Roulette. Craps. Baccarat.

Dice stickmen act as carnival barkers, touting the proposition bets. You soon become very conscious of the fact that you are at a table where the goal is *decisions*.

When the action is too decision-prone—too fast for you—walk away.

Look down at your ankles. There are no strings attached: no chains that bind you to stay at any table or in any casino twenty seconds longer than you feel you want to be there.

It's worth remembering.

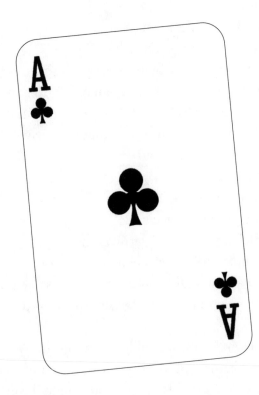

52

THE CASINO CONSUMER

There are casino veterans like myself who take an unusual position on casino profits.

We liken casinos to retailers who "sell" bets. And like the shops that market shoes or shirts at a profit, the casino, to survive, must "sell" its bets at a profit.

In other words, casinos don't win their money. They earn it.

Bill Friedman first offered this thesis in his classic book *Casino Management*.

Now comes the good part. Understand that casinos earn their money from winners rather than losers!

I'll explain it simply: You make $1,000 worth of wagers at craps. You lose. You didn't pay anything for the bets.

The casino could consider the thousand dollars it collected merely as money to be held in escrow. Another player will come along and place $1,000 on the crap tables and win.

Ah, here comes the moment of truth. When he wins, the casino gives him $1,000.

"What's wrong with that?" you may ask.

What's wrong is that if he were paid the true odds he would get approximately $1,028. This customer "paid" $28 for his bet.

One casino owner reports: "Customers are often a little flabbergasted when I tell them that I only make money when they win, not when they lose. This may be hard to believe, but nevertheless, it's true."

Let me quote further from Mr. Owner: "Simply winning a guy's money in the casino Doesn't give me any real satisfaction because that is just luck. I'm gambling, and I can't rely on it. The only thing I can rely on is what I earn, not what I win. What I happen to win on any given day is only escrow, and every casino's the same way. They only rely on what they earn from the house edge, that tiny 1.414 percent or .846 percent on the crap tables; that 5.26 percent on the roulette table, and so forth."

Here's another way of looking at the house edge. When a player makes a flat bet of $1,000 on the crap tables, the casino makes a $14 profit on that bet, whether the bettor wins or loses. They hold $14 in an imaginary escrow account. It's going to stay there, and they will be able to bank that money someday as sure as the sun is going to come up tomorrow.

"If the player makes ten bets at $1,000 a bet, that's $140 the casino earns. If he *wins* all ten bets, they still earn $140. He's ahead $10,000, but in actuality he's stuck 140 bucks because that's what those bets really cost him."

Bob Stupak of Vegas World subscribes to the above theory. He has said that most people know that, if you flip a coin, 50 percent of the time it's going to be heads. It might come up tails five times in a row, or even 100 times in a row, but we still know that in the long run, 50 percent of the time it's going to be heads.

"There might be big swings," says Stupak, "especially if a casino is dealing high. But the wins and the losses will balance out sooner or later, and so long as casinos take that commission, the house edge, from the winning bets, they are earning money. That's the only thing casinos care about—not what they win but what they earn."

When you win money in a casino, you've earned it. It's time to stop thinking about it as "their money" and it's probably time to run, not walk, to the nearest transportation home.

Remember the team motto: Hit-and-Run!

FINALE: YOUR GUIDE TO BEATING THE CASINO

Keep in mind that all gambling consists of taking a chance. Most things in life are matters of chance and circumstance—including whether lightning will strike you before tomorrow's sun rises in the east. Your winning must be measured against the consequences of possible loss. You *can* win. Whether you win or not often depends more on what *you* do than what cards and dice do.

You have the ingredients in this book that can change your play and alter the outcome.

Below are my now-legendary Nine Commandments. They've been copied and parodied. Indeed in the past nearly two decades, I rarely read a gaming book that doesn't "borrow" themes, ideas and advice from my first book. To the credit of some authors, they do often credit me.

Never forget that your first challenge is *you*. Control you, and you're several giant steps toward beating the casino.

It's possible, but *only you* can make it probable!
Luck to you!

THE NINE COMMANDMENTS

1. Never gamble when you are tired or unhappy.

2. Never gamble for more money than you can comfortably afford to lose.

3. Never forget that the longer you stay at any casino table, the larger are the odds that you will walk away a loser.

4. Never begin to play unless you know at exactly what loss point and/or win point you will quit.

5. Always place at least three-fourths of your winnings in a casino or hotel-provided safe deposit box. Refuse to gamble further if you lose the other 25 percent.

6. If you feel "negative," stop! Do other things until your mood changes. Depressed gamblers rarely win. And the tables are always there for when your attitudes/hunches change.

7. Avoid playing when you feel angry, insecure or lonely, or don't have a clear sense of discipline about a plan of action and a schedule of goals.

8. When on a losing streak, don't try to recoup by increasing the size of your wagers. On the contrary, cut them. Increase wagers when on a win streak. In other words, limit your losses but let your winnings run.

9. Always keep in mind that the real struggle isn't between you and the casino. It's between *you and yourself.*